PRAISE FOR
MARKETING ANALYTICS

'With its focus on practicality, this book is an invaluable toolkit of frameworks to drive consumer-centric analytics initiatives across marketing organizations. It is unique in going beyond theoretical aspects and helping practitioners apply analytics to understand consumer behaviour and identify business opportunities. Grigsby's extensive experience makes it a must-read for marketing professionals of all levels.' **Anna Andrusova, Senior Data Analyst, JCPenney**

'This is an excellent read for people in the industry who work in strategy and marketing. It is one of the first books that I have read that covers the entire spectrum from demand, segmentation, targeting, and how results can be calculated. In an age where marketing is becoming more and more sophisticated, this book provides the tools and the mathematics behind the facts. *Marketing Analytics* is written with a scientific voice, but is very readable, with the science wrapped into everyday activities, based on a character we can all relate to, that are derived from these formulas, ultimately driving ROI.' **Elizabeth Johnson, CEO, PathFormance**

'Grigsby's book is the right blend of theory applied to the real-world large-scale data problems of marketing. It's exactly the book I wish I'd had when I started out in this field.' **Jeff Weiner, Senior Director, Analytics, One10**

'An insightful, practical book for analytics marketing practitioners. It both entertains and serves as a handbook for marketing analytics. With easy-to-follow examples, Grigsby paints a clear picture of how to execute data analytics and its role in the larger marketing and organizational goals.' **Craig Armstrong, Director, Strategic Business Analysis, Targetbase**

'This is a great book for practitioners who have learned plenty of theories and want to learn how to apply methodologies. It is also a great, easy-to-read resource for anyone who does not have a deep theoretical background but wants to learn how analytics work in real life.' **Ingrid Guo, VP, Analytics, and Managing Director, Javelin Marketing Group (Beijing)**

'In *Marketing Analytics*, Mike Grigsby takes passionate marketing strategists on a practical, real-life journey for solving common marketing challenges. By combining the concepts and knowledge areas of statistics, marketing strategy and consumer behaviour, Grigsby recommends scientific and innovative solutions to common marketing problems in the current business environment. Every chapter is an interesting journey for the reader.

What I like most about the book is its simplicity and how it applies to real work-related situations in which almost all of us have been involved while practising marketing of any sort. I also like how the author talks about tangible measurements of strategic recommended marketing solutions as well as how they add value to companies' strategic endeavours. I highly recommend reading this book as it adds a completely new dimension to marketing science.'
Kristina Domazetoska, Project Manager and Implementation Consultant at Insala – Talent Development and Mentoring Solutions

'*Marketing Analytics*, second edition is a must-read for students and budding analytics professionals. The book illustrates concepts in statistics and marketing with real-world examples and provides solutions without getting too technical. It begins with basic statistical concepts required in the field of marketing analytics, then illustrates the application of these concepts to real-world business problems. It also touches upon concepts of big data analytics and, most importantly, what really IS an insight. This book is extremely conversational and entertaining to read and I've found myself reaching for it on multiple occasions when I've encountered various marketing-analytics-related problems, during both my student and professional life.' **Akshay Kher, Analytics Practitioner**

Second Edition

Marketing Analytics

A practical guide to improving consumer
insights using data techniques

Mike Grigsby

KoganPage

Publisher's note
Every possible effort has been made to ensure that the information contained in this book is accurate at the time of going to press, and the publisher and author cannot accept responsibility for any errors or omissions, however caused. No responsibility for loss or damage occasioned to any person acting, or refraining from action, as a result of the material in this publication can be accepted by the editor, the publisher or the author.

First published in Great Britain and the United States in 2015 by Kogan Page Limited as *Marketing Analytics: A practical guide to real marketing science*

Second edition published in 2018

Apart from any fair dealing for the purposes of research or private study, or criticism or review, as permitted under the Copyright, Designs and Patents Act 1988, this publication may only be reproduced, stored or transmitted, in any form or by any means, with the prior permission in writing of the publishers, or in the case of reprographic reproduction in accordance with the terms and licences issued by the CLA. Enquiries concerning reproduction outside these terms should be sent to the publishers at the undermentioned addresses:

2nd Floor, 45 Gee Street
London EC1V 3RS
United Kingdom

c/o Martin P Hill Consulting
122 W 27th St, 10th Floor
New York NY 10001
USA

4737/23 Ansari Road
Daryaganj
New Delhi 110002
India

www.koganpage.com

© Mike Grigsby, 2015, 2018

The right of Mike Grigsby to be identified as the author of this work has been asserted by him in accordance with the Copyright, Designs and Patents Act 1988.

ISBN   978 0 7494 8216 9
E-ISBN   978 0 7494 8217 6

British Library Cataloguing-in-Publication Data

A CIP record for this book is available from the British Library.

Library of Congress Cataloging-in-Publication Data
Names: Grigsby, Mike, author.
Title: Marketing analytics : a practical guide to improving consumer insights
   using data techniques / Mike Grigsby.
Description: Second edition. | London ; New York : Kogan Page, 2018. |
   Includes bibliographical references and index.
Identifiers: LCCN 2018004497 (print) | LCCN 2018003158 (ebook) | ISBN
   9780749482176 (ebook) | ISBN 9780749482169 (alk. paper)
Subjects: LCSH: Marketing research. | Marketing.
Classification: LCC HF5415.2 (print) | LCC HF5415.2 .G754 2018 (ebook) | DDC
   658.8/3–dc23

Typeset by Integra Software Services, Pondicherry
Print production managed by Jellyfish
Printed and bound by Ashford Colour Press Ltd

CONTENTS

06   When are my customers most likely to buy? 84

07   Panel regression – how to use a cross-sectional time series 100

Test banks, datasets and PowerPoint lecture slides relating to chapters are available online at: **www.koganpage.com/MarketingAnalytics2**

FOREWORD TO THE FIRST EDITION

In *Marketing Analytics* Mike Grigsby provides a new way of thinking about solving marketing and business problems, with a practical set of solutions. This relevant guide is intended for practitioners across a variety of fields, but is rigorous enough to satisfy the appetite of scholars as well.

I can certainly appreciate Mike's motivations for the book. This book is his way of giving back to the analytics community by offering advice and step-by-step guidance for ways to solve some of the most common situations, opportunities, and problems in marketing. He knows what works for entry, mid-level, and very experienced career analytics professionals, because this is the kind of guide he would have liked at these stages.

While Mike's education includes a PhD in Marketing Science, he also pulls from his vast experiences from his start as an Analyst, through his journey to VP of Analytics, to walk the reader through the types of questions and business challenges we face in the analytics field on a regular basis. His authority on the subject matter is obvious, and his enthusiasm is contagious, and best captured by my favourite sentence of his book: 'Now let's look at some data and run a model, because that's where all the fun is.'

What this education and experience means for the rest of us is that we have a well-informed author providing us with insight into the realities of what is needed from the exciting work we do, and how we can not only provide better decision making, but also move the needle on important theoretical and methodological approaches in Analytics.

More specifically, *Marketing Analytics* covers both inter-relational and dependency-driven analytics and modelling to solve marketing problems. In a light and conversational style (both engaging and surprising) Mike argues that, ultimately, all markets rely on a strong understanding of the ever-changing, difficult to predict, sometimes fuzzy, and elusive minds and hearts of consumers. Anything we can do to better arm ourselves as marketers to develop this understanding is certainly time well spent. Consumers can and should be the focal point of great strategy, operational standards of excellence and processes, tactical decisions, product design, and so much more, which is why it makes perfect sense to better understand not just consumer behaviours, but also consumer thoughts, opinions, and feelings, particularly related to your vertical, competitors, and brand.

After a review of seminal work on consumer behaviour, and an overview of general statistics and statistical techniques, *Marketing Analytics* dives into realistic business scenarios with the clever use of corporate dialogue between Scott, our fictitious analyst, and his boss. As our protagonist progresses through his career, we see an improvement in his toolkit of analytical techniques. He moves from an entry level analyst in a cubicle to a senior leader of analytics with staff. The problems become more challenging, and the process for choosing the analytics to apply to the situations presented is an uncanny reflection of reality – at least based on my experiences.

What I appreciate absolutely most about this work though is the full spectrum of problem solving, not just analytics in a vacuum. Mike walks us from the initial moment when a problem is identified, through communication of that problem, framing by the Analytics team, technique selection and execution (from the straightforward to somewhat advanced), communication of results, and usefulness to the company. This rare and certainly more complete picture warrants a title such as Problem Solving using Marketing Analytics in lieu of the shorter title Mike chose.

Marketing Analytics will have you rethinking your methods, developing more innovative ways to progress your marketing analytics techniques, and adjusting your communication practices. Finally, a book we all can use!

Dr Beverly Wright, VP, Analytics, BKV Consulting

FOREWORD TO THE SECOND EDITION

Mike Grigsby has done the seemingly impossible: created a guide to marketing analytics that is technically sound and clearly applicable to real-world business cases, while also being a thoroughly enjoyable (and even entertaining!) read.

The first edition of *Marketing Analytics* was so well received by educators and practitioners because it delivered simple, straightforward analytic prescriptions to those seeking an actionable primer. In a market that remains largely saturated with jargon-laced statistical tomes geared more towards academicians than to marketers, the second edition of *Marketing Analytics* continues to distinguish itself as the user-friendly text that earns the coveted 'quick reach' spot on analysts' office bookshelves. Mike serves up new chapters on panel regression and big data analytics, with these (and all other covered techniques) framed and contextualized by a thoughtful new overview chapter that addresses a basic – but often elusive – question: 'What is an Insight?'

The book is logically structured, with a clear progression from foundational principles to workhorse techniques in predictive modelling (dependent variable applications) and segmentation (inter-relationship solutions), concluding with treatments of some of the most important topics in the field, including the pivotal role of consumer behaviour, the logic of testing and inference and the rise of big data solutions. In short, this edition covers the lion's share of methods used by successful marketing analysts, and it should be required reading for students and marketers alike.

A number of admirable traits define the discussion of the subject matter. First, the description of core topics is informative and practical. Each method contains a clear description of when and why it is used, with key diagnostics and test statistics presented in practical, lay terms. In addition, the treatment of each topic is illustrative, following the career trajectory of our protagonist, Scott, as he confronts and addresses increasingly complex business problems over the course of his career. (The dialogue-laden narratives are refreshing, making the material more accessible to – and more fun for – the book's diverse audience.) Further illustrations to each technique are provided by 'highlight' sections in which Mike presents case vignettes of how he actually applied these techniques to answer business questions over the course of his career. Finally, the book is to be commended for adopting a consumer-centric point of view on applied analytics. Mike correctly challenges his readers to don the mental mantle of the customer, tailoring analytic choices to focus on how and why customers make decisions and how we as marketers can impact those decisions.

I am fortunate to have Dr Grigsby join our Consumer Insights practice at Brierley & Partners. I can attest that Mike practises what he preaches in his book, and he is a patient mentor to his analysts and a trusted advisor to many of our largest clients.

As the field of marketing analytics continues to explode, aspiring practitioners and veteran analysts would do well to ensure that their solutions are grounded in the customer-centric approaches delineated in this work. As new touch points and information sources continue to crowd and compete for attention in the modern marketing ecosystem, analytics would be wise to heed Mike's astute observation: 'Generally speaking, new data sources do not require new analytic techniques.' What is required is an action-oriented approach to using analytics to meaningfully impact customer choice – a framework cleanly served up in this second edition of *Marketing Analytics*.

Don Smith, PhD, Chief Analytics Officer, Brierley & Partners

PREFACE

We'll start by trying to get a few things straight. I did not set out to write a (typical) textbook. I'll mention some textbooks down the line that might be helpful in some areas, but this is too slim for an academic tome. Leaf through it and you'll not find any mathematical proofs, nor are there pages upon pages of equations. This is meant to be a gentle overview – more conceptual than statistical – for the marketing analyst who just needs to know how to get on with their job. That is, it's for those who are, or hope to be, practitioners. This is written with practitioners in mind.

Introduction to marketing analytics

Who is the intended audience for this book?

This is not meant to be an academic tome filled with mathematical minutia and cluttered with statistical mumbo-jumbo. There will need to be an equation now and then, but if your interest is econometric rigour, you're in the wrong place. A couple of good books for that are *Econometric Analysis* by William H Greene (1993) and *Econometric Models, Techniques and Applications* by Michael Intriligator, Ronald G Bodkin and Cheng Hsiao (1996). So, this book is not aimed at the statistician, although there will be a fair amount of verbiage about statistics.

This is not meant to be a replacement for a programming manual, even though there will be SAS code sprinkled in now and then. If you're all about BI (business intelligence), which means mostly reporting and visualizing data, this is not for you.

This will not be a marketing strategy guide, but be aware that as mathematics is the handmaiden of science, marketing analytics is the handmaiden of marketing strategy. There is no point to analytics unless it has a strategic payoff. It's not what is interesting to the analyst, but what is impactful to the business that is the focus of marketing science.

So, at whom is this book aimed? Not necessarily at the professional econometrician/statistician, but there ought to be some satisfaction here for them. Primarily, the aim is at the practitioner (or those who will be). The intended audience is the business analyst that has to pull a targeted list, the campaign manager that needs to know which promotion worked best, the marketer that must DE-market some segment of her customers to gain efficiency, the marketing researcher that needs to design and implement a satisfaction survey, the pricing analyst that has to set optimal prices between products and brands, etc.

What is marketing science?

As alluded to above, marketing science is the analytic arm of marketing. Marketing science (interchangeable with marketing analytics) seeks to quantify causality. Marketing science is not an oxymoron (like military intelligence, happily married or jumbo shrimp) but is a necessary (although not sufficient) part of marketing strategy. It is more than simply designing campaign test cells. Its overall purpose is to decrease the chance of marketers making a wrong decision. It cannot replace managerial judgement, but it can offer boundaries and guard rails to inform strategic decisions. It encompasses areas from marketing research all the way to database marketing.

Why is marketing science important?

Marketing science quantifies the causality of consumer behaviour. If you don't know already, consumer behaviour is the centre-point, the hub, the pivot around which all marketing hinges. Any 'marketing' that is not about consumer behaviour (understanding it, incentivizing it, changing it, etc) is probably heading down the wrong road.

Marketing science gives input/information to the organization. This information is necessary for the very survival of the firm. Much like an organism requires information from its environment in order to change, adapt and evolve, an organization needs to know how its operating environment changes. To not collect and act and evolve based on this information would be death. To survive, for both the organization and the organism, insights (from data) are required. Yes, this is reasoning by analogy but you see what I mean.

Marketing science teases out strategy. Unless you know what causes what, you will not know which lever to pull. Marketing science tells you, for instance, that this segment is sensitive to price, this cohort prefers this marcom (marketing communication) vehicle, this group is under competitive pressure, this population is not loyal, and so on. Knowing which lever to pull (by different consumer groups) allows optimization of your portfolio.

What kind of people in what jobs use marketing science?

Most people in marketing science (also called decision science, analytics, customer relationship management – or CRM, direct/database marketing, insights, research, etc) have a quantitative bent. Their education is typically some combination involving statistics, econometrics/economics, mathematics, programming/computer science, business/marketing/marketing research, strategy, intelligence, operations, etc. Their experience certainly touches any and all parts of the above. The ideal analytic person has a strong quantitative orientation as well as a feel for consumer behaviour and the strategies that affect it. As in all marketing, consumer behaviour is the focal point of marketing science.

Marketing science is usually practised in firms that have a CRM or direct/database marketing component, or firms that do marketing research and need to undertake analytics on the survey responses. Forecasting is a part of marketing science, as well as design of experiments (DOE), web analytics and even choice behaviour (conjoint). In short, any quantitative analysis applied to economic/marketing data will have a marketing science application. So while the subjects of analysis are fairly broad, the number of (typical) analytic techniques tends to be fairly narrow. See *Consumer Insight* by Stone, Bond and Foss (2004) to get a view of this in action.

Why do I think I have something to say about marketing science?

Fair question. My whole career has been involved in marketing analytics. For more than 25 years I've done direct marketing, CRM, database marketing, marketing research, decision sciences, forecasting, segmentation, design of experiments and all the rest. While my BBA and MBA are in finance, my PhD is in marketing science. I've published a few trade and academic articles, I've taught school at both graduate and undergraduate levels and I've spoken at conferences, all involved in marketing science. I've done all this for firms like Dell, HP, the Gap and Sprint, as well as consultancies like Targetbase and Brierley + Partners. Over the years I've gathered a few opinions that I'd like to share with y'all. And yes, I've been in Texas for over 15 years.

What is the approach/philosophy of this book?

As with most non-fiction writers, I wrote this because I would have loved to have had it, or something like it, earlier. What I had in mind did not actually exist, as far as I knew.

I had been a practitioner for decades and there were times I just wanted to know what I should do, what analytic technique would best solve the problem I had. I did not need a mathematically-oriented econometrics textbook (like Greene's, or Kmenta's *Elements of Econometrics* (1986) as great as they each are). I did not need a list of statistical techniques (like *Multivariate Data Analysis* by Hair *et al* (1998) or *Multivariate Statistical Analysis* by Sam Kash Kachigan (1991)) as great as each of them also are. What I needed was a (simple) explanation of which technique would address the marketing problem I was working on. I wanted something direct, accessible, and easy to understand so I could use it and then explain it. It was okay if the book went into more technical details later, but first I needed something conceptual to guide in solving a particular problem. What I needed was a marketing-focused book explaining how to use statistical/econometric techniques on marketing problems. It would be ideal if it showed examples and case studies doing just that. Voila.

Generally this book has the same point of view as books like Peter Kennedy's *A Guide to Econometrics* (1998) and Glenn L Urban and Steven H Star's *Advanced Marketing Strategy* (1991). That is, the techniques will be described in two or three levels. The first is really just conceptual, devoid of mathematics, and the aim is to understand. The next level is more technical, and will use SAS or something else as needed to illustrate what is involved, how to interpret it, etc. Then the final level, if there is one, will be rather technical and aimed really only at the professional. And there will be business cases to offer examples of how analytics solves marketing questions.

One thing I like about Stephan Sorger's 2013 book, *Marketing Analytics*, is that in the opening pages he champions action-ability. Marketing science has to be about action-ability. I know some academic purists will read the following pages and gasp that I occasionally allow 'bad stats' to creep in. (For example, it is well known that forecasting often is improved if collinear independent variables are found. Shock!) But the point is that even an imperfect model is far more valuable than waiting for academic white tower purity. Business is about time and money and even a cloudy insight can help improve targeting. Put simply, this book, and marketing science, is ultimately about what works, not what will be published in an academic research paper.

All of the above will be cast in terms of business problems, that is, in terms of marketing questions. For example, a marketer, say, needs to target his market and he has to learn to do segmentation. Or she has to manage a group that will do segmentation for her (a consultant) and needs to know something about it in order to intelligently question. The problem will be addressed in terms of what is segmentation, what does it mean to strategy, why do it, etc. Then a description of several analytic techniques used for segmentation will be detailed. Then a fairly involved and technical discussion will show more additional statistical output, and an example or two will be shown. This output will use SAS (or SPSS, etc) as necessary. This will also help guide students as they prepare to become analysts.

Therefore, the philosophy is to present a business case (a need to answer the marketing questions) and describe conceptually various marketing science techniques (in two or three increasingly detailed levels) that can answer those questions. Then with, say, SAS, output will be developed that shows how the technique works, how to interpret it and how to use it to solve the business problem. Finally, more technical details may be shown, as needed. Okay?

So, on to a little statistical review.

PART ONE
Overview

How can marketing analytics help you?

A brief statistics review

You knew we had to do this, have a general review of basic statistics. I promise, it'll be mostly conceptual, a gentle reminder of what we learned in Introductory Statistics. Also note the definition boxes helping to describe key terms, point out jargon, etc.

Measures of central tendency

First we'll deal with simple descriptive statistics, confined to one variable. We'll start with measures of central tendency.

Measures of central tendency include the mean, median and mode.

Mean: a descriptive statistic, a measure of central tendency, the mean is a calculation summing up the value of all the observations and dividing by the number of observations.

The mean is calculated as:

$$\bar{X} = \frac{\sum xi}{n}$$

That is, sum all the observations up (all the individual Xs) and then divide by the number of observations (Xs). This is commonly called 'the average' but I'd like to offer a different view of 'average'.

> **Average**: the most representative measure of central tendency, NOT necessarily the mean.

Average is the measure of central tendency, the number most likely to occur, the most representative number. That is, it might not be the mean; it could be the median or even the mode. This is our first incursion into a statistical way of thinking.

I'd like to persuade you that it's possible, for example, that the median is more representative than the mean, in some cases – and that in those cases the median is the average, the most representative number.

> **Median**: the middle observation in an odd number of observations, or the mean of the middle two observations.

The median is, by definition, the number in the middle, the 50th percentile, that value that has just as many observations above it as below it.

Consider home sales prices via Figure 1.1. The mean is 141,000 but the median is 110,000. Which number is most representative? I submit it is not

Figure 1.1   Home sales prices

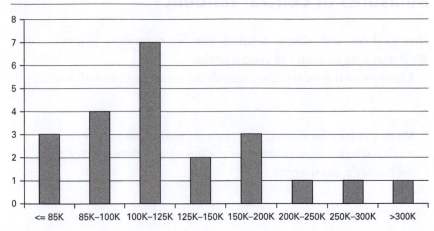

the mean, but the median. I also submit that the best measure of central tendency, in this example, is the median. Therefore the median is the average. I know that's not what you learned in third grade, but get used to it. Statistics has a way of turning one slightly askew.

Just to be clear, I suggest that the measure of central tendency that best describes the histogram above should be called 'average'. Mode is the number that appears most often, median is the observation in the middle and mean is the observations summed over their count.

> **Mode:** the number that appears most often.

Average is the most representative number. Of course it doesn't help this argument that Excel uses =AVERAGE( ) as the function to calculate the mean instead of =MEAN( ). I've tried asking Bill about it but he's not returned my calls, so far.

Measures of dispersion

Measures of central tendency alone do not adequately describe the variable (a variable is a thing that varies, like home sales prices). The other dimension of a variable is dispersion, or spread.

There are three measures of dispersion: range, variance and standard deviation.

> **Range:** a measure of dispersion or spread, calculated as the maximum value less the minimum value.

Range is easy. It's simply the minimum (smallest value) observation subtracted from the maximum (largest value). It's not particularly useful, especially in a marketing context.

Variance is another measure of dispersion or spread.

> **Variance:** a measure of spread, calculated as the summed square of each observation less the mean, divided by the count of observations less one.

Conceptually it takes each observation and subtracts the mean of all the observations from it, then squares each observation and adds up the squares.

That quantity is divided by $n-1$, the total number of observations, less one. The formula is below. Note this is the sample formula, not the formula for the population.

$$S^2 = \Sigma \frac{(X_i - \bar{X})^2}{n-1}$$

(Note that X-bar is the symbol for sample mean, while μ would be the symbol to use for population mean; s would be the symbol to use for sample standard deviation and σ would be the symbol to use for population standard deviation.)

Now, what does variance tell us? Unfortunately, not much. It says that (from Table 1.1) this variable of 18 observations has a mean of 25 and a

Table 1.1 Variance

X	X-mean	Squared
2	−23	529.3
5	−20	400.3
8	−17	289.2
10.9	−14.1	199.3
13.9	−11.1	123.6
16.9	−8.1	65.9
19.9	−5.1	26.2
22.9	−2.1	4.5
25.9	0.9	0.8
28.9	3.9	15.1
31.9	6.9	47.4
33	8	63.9
34	9	80.9
35	10	99.9
36	11	120.9
39	14	195.8
42	17	288.8
45	20	399.7
Mean = 25.0 Count = 18		Sum = 2,951.5 Variance = 173.6

variance, or spread, of 173.6. But variance gets us to the standard deviation, which DOES mean something.

Standard deviation: the square root of variance.

Standard deviation is calculated by taking the square root of variance. In this case the square root of 173.6 is 13.17. Now, what does 13.17 mean? It describes spread or dispersion in a way that removes the scale of the variable. That is, there are known qualities of a standard deviation. In a fairly normal distribution dispersion is spread around the mean (which equals the mode which equals the median). That is, there is a symmetrical spread around the mean of 25. In this case the spread is 25 +/– 13.17. That means that, in general, one standard deviation (+/– 13.17) from the mean will contain 68% of all observations: see Figure 1.2. That is, as the count increases (based on the central limit theorem) the distribution approaches normal. In a normal (bell-shaped) curve, 50% of all observations fall to the left of the mean and 50% of all observations fall to the right of the mean. Knowing the standard deviation gives information about the variable that cannot be obtained any other way.

Figure 1.2   Standard deviation

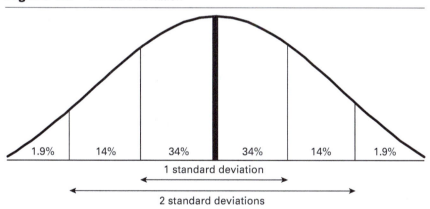

So, by saying a variable has a mean of 25 and a standard deviation of 13.17, automatically means that 68% of all observations are between 11.8 and 38.2. This immediately tells me that if I find an observation that is < 11.8, it is a little rare, or unusual, given that 68% will be > 11.8 (and < 38.2).

So, one standard deviation accounts for 34% below the mean and 34% above the mean. The second standard deviation accounts for 14% and the third deviation accounts for almost 1.99%. This means that three stand-ard deviations to the left of the mean accounts for 34% + 14% + 1.99%, or nearly 50% of all observations. Likewise for the positive/right side of the mean.

As an example, it is well known that IQ has a mean of 100 and a standard deviation of about 15. This means that 34% of the population should fall between 100 and 115. This is because the mean is 100 and the standard deviation is 15, or 115. The second standard deviation accounts for another 14%. Or 48% (34% + 14%) of the population should be between 100 and 130. Finally, just under 2% will be > 3 standard deviation, or having an IQ > 130. So you see how useful the standard deviation is. It immediately gives more information about the spread, or how likely or unusual particular observations are. For example, if we had an IQ test that showed 150, this is a VERY rare event, in that it's in the realm of > 4 standard deviations: 100–115 is 1, 115–130 is 2, 145 is 3 and 150 is 3.33 standard deviations above the mean.

The normal distribution

I've already mentioned the normal distribution but let's say a couple more clarifying things about it. The normal distribution is the traditional bell-shaped curve. One characteristic of a normal distribution is that the mean and the median and the mode are virtually the same number. The normal distribution is symmetrical about the measure of central tendency (mean, median and mode) and the standard deviation describes the spread, as above.

Let's also mention the central limit theorem. This simply means that as n, or the count, increases, the distribution approaches a normal distribution. This allows us to treat all variables as normal.

Now for a quick word about z-scores as this will be handy later.

Z-score: a metric describing how many standard deviations an observation is from its mean.

A z-score is a measure of the number of standard deviations an observation is relative to its mean. It converts

$$\text{z-score} = \frac{(X_i - \bar{X})}{s}$$

an observation, into the number of standard deviations above or below the mean by taking the observation (X_i) and subtracting the mean from it and then dividing that quantity by its standard deviation. In terms of IQ, an observation of 107.5 will have a z-score of (107.5 – 100)/15, or 0.5. This means that an IQ of 107.5 is one-half a standard deviation above the mean. Since 34% (from 100–115) lie above the mean, a z-score of 0.5 means this observation occurs half way, or about 17%, above the mean. This means this observation is 17% above average (which is 50%) or greater than 67% of the population. Note that 17% + 14% + 1.99% (or about 33%) are above this observation.

Confidence intervals

Another important measure to know about is the confidence interval. As opposed to a point estimate (which we will mostly do going forward), a confidence interval is an interval estimate. It tells the range of likely observations, given the metrics variance.

The formula for a confidence interval is:

$$CI = \bar{x} +/- z\left(\frac{s}{\sqrt{n}}\right)$$

This gives an upper and a lower limit. It takes the mean and then adds and subtracts the z-value (for 95% that would be 1.96) and multiplies by the standard error, which is the square root of the standard deviation divided by the square root of n, the number of observations.

Say we want to know the 95% confidence interval of 16 IQ scores collected. The standard deviation of those scores is 225. (Surprised?) To compute that confidence interval:

$$CI = 100 +/- 1.96\left(\frac{225}{\sqrt{16}}\right) = [92.65 - 107.35]$$

Which means 68% of expected IQ scores will be between 92.65 and 107.35.

Note the difference in the denominator between z-scores and confidence intervals. The z-score has the standard deviation, s, as the denominator and the confidence interval has se, which is an estimate of s, as the denominator.

Relations among two variables: covariance and correlation

All of the above descriptive discussions were about one variable. Remember that a variable is an item that takes on multiple values. That is, a variable is a thing that varies. Now let's talk about having two variables and the descriptive measures of them.

Covariance

Covariance, like variance, is how one variable varies in terms of another variable.

> **Covariance:** the dispersion or spread of two variables.

It, like variance, does not mean much; it's just a number. It has no scale, nor boundaries, and interpretation is minimal. The formula is:

$$\text{Covar}_{xy} = \frac{\Sigma(X_i - \bar{x})(Y_i - \bar{y})}{n}$$

It merely describes how each X observation varies from its mean, in terms of how each Y observation varies from its mean. Then sum these up and divide by n, the count. Again, the number is nearly irrelevant.

Say we have the dataset in Table 1.2. Note the covariance is 77.05, which again means very little.

Correlation

Correlation, like standard deviation, does have a meaning, and an important one.

> **Correlation:** a measure of both strength and direction, calculated as the covariance of X and Y divided by the standard deviation of X* the standard deviation of Y.

Correlation expresses both strength and direction of the two variables. It ranges from −100% to +100%. A negative correlation means that as, say,

Table 1.2 Covariance and correlation

X	Y
2	3
4	5
6	7
8	9
9	9
11	11
11	8
13	10
15	12
17	14
19	16
21	22
22	22
24	11
26	12
28	22
30	24
32	26
33	28
33	39
Covar =	77.05
Correl =	87.90%

X goes up, Y tends to go down. A very strong positive correlation (say 80% or 90%) means that as X goes up by, say 10, Y also goes up by nearly the same amount, maybe 8 or 9. Note that in Table 1.2 the correlation is 87.9% which is probably a very strong relationship between X and Y. The formula for correlation is covariance of X and Y divided by the standard deviation of X* the standard deviation of Y. That is, to go from covariance to correlation, covariance is divided by the standard deviation of x multiplied by the standard deviation of y. The formula is:

$$\rho = \frac{Covar(x,y)}{SxSy}$$

Probability and the sampling distribution

Probability is an important concept in statistics of course and I'll only touch on it here.

First, let's talk about two kinds of thinking: deductive and inductive. Deductive thinking is what you are most familiar with: based on rules of logic and conclusions from causality. Because of this thing, this conclusion must be true. However, statistical thinking is inductive, not deductive. Inductive thinking reasons from sample to population. That is, statistics is about inferences and generalizing the conclusion. This is where probability comes in. Typically, in marketing, we never have the whole population of a dataset: we have a sample.

Here's where it gets a little theoretical. Say we have a sample of data on X that contains 1,000 observations with a mean of 50. Now, theoretically, we could have an infinite number of samples that have a variety of means. Indeed, we never know where our sample is (with its mean of 50) in the total possibility of samples. If we did have a large number of samples drawn from the population and we calculated those means of those samples that would constitute a sampling distribution.

For example, say we have a barrel containing 100,000 marbles. That is the whole population. 10% of these marbles are red and 90% of these marbles are white. We can only draw a sample of 100 at a time and calculate the mean of red marbles.

In this case (contrived as it is) we KNOW the average number of marbles drawn, overall, will be 10%. But note – and this is important – there is no guarantee that any one of our samples of 100 will actually be 10%. It could be 5% (3.39% of the time it will be) and it could be 14% (5.13% of the time it will be). It will, of course, on average, be 10%. Indeed, only 13.19% of the sample drawn will actually be 10%! The binomial distribution tells us the above facts.

Therefore, we could have drawn an unusual sample that had only 5% red marbles. This would occur 3.39% of the time, roughly 1 out of 33. That's not that rare. And we have in actuality no way to really know how likely the sample we have is to contain the population mean of 10%. This is where confidence intervals come in, which we discussed earlier in this chapter.

Conclusion

That's all I want to mention in terms of statistical background. More will be applied later. Now let's get on with the fun.

Checklist

You'll be the smartest person in the room if you:

- ☐ Remember three measures of central tendency: mean, median and mode.

- ☐ Remember three measures of dispersion: range, variance and standard deviation.

- ☐ Constantly point out the real definition of average as 'the most representative number', that is, it might NOT necessarily be the mean.

- ☐ Always look at a metric in terms of both central tendency as well as dispersion.

- ☐ Think of a z-score as a measure of the likelihood of an observation occurring.

- ☐ Observe that correlation is about two dimensions: strength and direction.

Brief principles of consumer behaviour and marketing strategy 02

Introduction

You will note that I have tied two subjects together in this chapter: consumer behaviour and marketing strategy. That's because marketing strategy is all about understanding consumer behaviour and incentivizing it in such a way that the firm and the consumer both win. I know a lot of marketers will be saying, 'But what about competitors? Are they not part of marketing strategy?' And the answer is, 'No, not really.' I am aware of the gasps this will cause.

By understanding consumer behaviour, part of that insight will come from what experience consumers have with competitors, but the focus is on consumer, not competitive, behaviour. I know John Nash and his work in game theory takes a back seat in my view, but this is on purpose. Much like the financial motto 'watch the pennies and the dollars will follow', I say, 'focus on the consumer and competitive understanding will follow'.

Just to be clear, marketing science should be at the consumer level, NOT the competitive level. By focusing on competitors you automatically move from a marketing point of view toward a financial/economic point of view.

Consumer behaviour as the basis for marketing strategy

In marketing, the consumer is central

I like to use Steven P Schnaars' *Marketing Strategy* because of the focus on consumer behaviour (Schnaars, 1997). And because he's right. A marketing orientation is consumer-centric; anything else is by definition NOT marketing. Marketing drives financial results and in order to be marketing-oriented there must be a consumer-centric focus. That means all marketing activities are geared to learn and understand consumer (and ultimately customer) behaviour.

The marketing concept does not mean giving the consumer (only) what they want, because:

1 the consumer's wants can be widely divergent;

2 the consumer's wants contradict the firm's minimum needs; and

3 the consumer might not know what they want. It is marketing's job to learn and understand and incentivize consumer behaviour to a win-win position.

The objection from product-centric marketers

As a fair argument, consumer-centricity runs contra to product managers. Product managers focus on developing products and THEN finding consumers to buy them. (Immediate examples that spring to mind come from technology, such as original HP, Apple, etc.) This sometimes works, but often it does not. The poster child for product focus regardless of what consumers think they want is Chrysler's minivan strategy. The story is that Chrysler chief Lee Iacocca wanted to design and produce the minivan but the market research they did told him there was no demand for it. Consumers were confused by the 'half way between a car and a conversion (full-size) van' and were not interested in it. Iacocca went ahead and designed and built it and it basically saved Chrysler. What is the point? One point is that consumers do not always know what they want, especially with a new/innovative product they have no experience with. The second point is that not everyone has the genius of Lee Iacocca.

Overview of consumer behaviour

Background of consumer behaviour

A simple view of consumer behaviour is best understood in the micro-economic analysis of 'the consumer problem'. This is generally summarized in three questions:

1 What are consumers' preferences (in terms of goods/services)?

2 What are consumers' constraints (allocating limited budgets)?

3 Given limited resources, what are consumers' choices?

This assumes that consumers are rational and have a desire to maximize their satisfaction.

Let's talk about general assumptions of consumer preferences. The first is that preferences are complete, meaning consumers can compare and rank all products. The second assumption is that preferences are transitive. This is the mathematical requirement that if X is preferred to Y and Y is preferred to Z then X is preferred to Z. The third assumption is that products are desirable (a 'good' is good or of value). This means that more is better (costs notwithstanding).

A quick look into the assumptions above makes it clear that they are made in order to do the mathematics. This ultimately means that curves will be produced (the bane of most microeconomics students) that lend themselves to simple graphics. This immediately leads into using the calculus for analytic reasons. Calculus requires smooth curves and twice differentiability in order to work. THIS means that some heroic assumptions indeed are required, especially *ceteris paribus* (holding all other things constant).

The decision process

Consumers go through a shopping–purchasing process, using decision analytics to come to a choice. It should be recognized that not all decisions are equally important or complex. Based on the risk of a wrong choice, either extended problem solving or limited problem solving will tend to be used.

Extended problem solving is used when the cost of the product is high, or the product will be lived with for a long time, or it's the initial purchase, etc. Something about the choice requires more thought, evaluation and rigour.

Limited problem solving is of course the opposite. When products are inexpensive, short lived, not really important or with low risk of a 'wrong' decision, limited problem solving is used. Often one or more of the (below) steps are omitted. The choice is more automatic. The choice is usually reduced to a rule: what experience the consumer has had before, what brand they have disliked, what price is low enough, what their neighbours have told them, etc.

The typical decision process in terms of consumer behaviour (for example, see *Consumer Behavior* by Engel, Blackwell and Miniard, 1995) is about need recognition, search for information, information processing, alternative evaluation, purchase and post-purchase evaluation. There are marketing opportunities along each step to influence and incentivize.

Need recognition

The initiator of the consumer decision process is need recognition. This is a realization that there is a 'cognitive dissonance' between some ideal state and the current state. There is much advertising around need arousal. From educating consumers on real needs (survival, satisfaction) to informing consumers about pseudo-needs ('jump on the bandwagon – all of your friends have already done it!') need arousal is where it starts.

Search for information

Now the consumer recalls what they have heard or what they know about the product to infer, depending on whether the product requires limited or extensive engagement, an ability to make a decision. Obviously advertising and branding come into play here, informing consumers of benefits, differentiation, etc.

Information processing

The next step is for the consumer to absorb what information they have and what facts they know. Most marketing messaging strategies prefer for consumers to NOT process information, but to recall such things as positive brand exposure, satisfaction from previous interactions or emotional loyalty. If consumers do not 'process' information (ie, critically evaluate costs and benefits) then they can use brand equity/satisfaction to make the shorthand decision. It is marketing science's job to find those that are considering, distinct from those that have 'already decided'.

Pre-purchase alternative evaluation

Now, after information has been processed, comes the critical final comparison: does the potential product have attributes the consumer considers greater than the consumer's standards? That is, given budgetary standards, what is the product likely to offer in terms of satisfaction (economic utilization) after the consumer has decided it is above minimum qualifications?

Purchase

Finally, the whole point of the marketing funnel is purchase. A sale is the last piece. This is the decision of the consumer based on the shopping process described above. The actual purchase action carries within it all the above (and below) processes and all of the actual and perceived product attributes.

Post-purchase evaluation

But the consumer decision process does not (usually) end with purchase. Generally it is a comparison with what the consumer thought (hoped) would be the utilization gained from consuming the product compared to what actual (perceived) satisfaction was received from the product. That is, the creation of loyalty starts post purchase.

Now, with consumer behaviour centrally located, let's think about a firm's strategy. Keep the differences between competitive moves and consumer behaviour firmly in mind.

Overview of marketing strategy

The above focused on consumer behaviour. Marketing, to be marketing, is about understanding and incentivizing consumer behaviour in such a way that both the consumer and the firm get what they want. Consumers want a product that they need when they need it at a price that gives them value through a channel they prefer. Firms want loyalty, customer satisfaction and growth. Since a market is a place where buyers and sellers meet, marketing is the function that moves the buyers and sellers toward each other.

Given the above, it should be noted that marketing strategy has evolved (primarily via microeconomics) to a firm vs firm rivalry. That is, marketing strategy is in danger of forgetting the focus on consumer behaviour and jumping deep into something like game theory wherein one firm competes with another firm.

Everything that follows about marketing strategy can be thought of as an indirect consequence of firm vs firm based on a direct consequence of focusing on consumer behaviour. That is, fighting a firm means incentivizing consumers. Think of it as an iceberg: what is seen (firms competing) is the tip above the surface, but what is really happening that moves the iceberg is unseen (from other firm's point of view) below the surface (incentivizing consumers).

Types of marketing strategy

Everyone should be aware of Michael Porter and his monumental article and book about competitive strategy (Porter, 1979/1980). This is where marketing strategy became a discipline.

First Porter detailed factors creating competitive intensity. (To make an obvious point: what are firms competing over? Consumer loyalty.) These factors are the bargaining power of suppliers, the bargaining power of buyers, the threat of new entrants, the rivalry among existing firms and the threat of substitute products:

The **bargaining power of buyers** means firms lose profit from powerful buyers demanding lower prices. This means consumers are sensitive to price.

The **bargaining power of suppliers** means firms lose profit due to potential increased factor (input) prices. Suppliers only have bargaining power because a firm's margins are low, because a firm cannot raise prices, because consumers are sensitive to price.

The **threat of new entrants** lowers profits due to new competitors entering the market. Again, consumers are sensitive to price and very informed about the other firm's offerings.

The **intensity of rivalry** causes lower prices because of the zero sum game supplied by consumers. There are only a certain number of potential loyal customers and if a firm gains one then another firm loses that one.

The **threat of substitute products** invites consumers to choose among the lower-priced products.

Note how all of this strategy (which appears like firms fighting other firms) is actually based on consumer behaviour. Am I putting too fine a point on this? Maybe, but it does help us focus, right?

Based on these factors a firm can ascertain the intensity of competition. The more competitive the industry is, the more a firm must be a price taker, that is, they have little market power, meaning little control over price.

This affects the amount of profit each firm in the industry can expect. Given this, a firm can evaluate their strengths and weaknesses and decide how to compete. Or not.

Porter then did a brilliant thing: he devised, based on the above, three generic strategies. A firm can compete on costs (be the low-cost provider), a firm can differentiate and focus on high-end products or a firm can segment and focus on a smaller, niche part of the market. The point is the firm needs to create and adhere to a particular strategy. Often firms are diluted and do everything at once.

However, Treacy and Wiersema took Porter's framework and evolved it (Treacy and Wiersema, 1997). They too came up with three strategies (disciplines): operational excellence (basically a focus on lower costs), product leadership (a focus on higher-end differentiated products) and customer intimacy (a differentiation/segmentation strategy). You can see their use and extension of Porter's ideas. Both have the same bottom line: firms should be disciplined and concentrate their efforts corporate-wide on primarily one (and only one) strategic focus.

Applied to consumer behaviour

Stephan Sorger's excellent *Marketing Analytics* (Sorger, 2013) has a brief description of competitive moves, both offensive and defensive. Summaries of each move but applied via consumer behaviour are now considered.

Defensive reactions to competitor moves

Bypass attack (the attacking firm expands into one of our product areas) and the correct counter is for us to constantly explore new areas. Remember Theodore Levitt's 'Marketing myopia' (Levitt, 1960)? If not, re-read it; you know you had to in school.

Encirclement attack (the attacking firm tries to overpower us with larger forces) and the correct counter is to message how our products are superior/unique and of more value. This requires a constant monitoring of message effectiveness.

Flank attack (the attacking firm tries to exploit our weaknesses) and the correct counter is to not have any weaknesses. This again requires monitoring and messaging the uniqueness/value of our products.

Frontal attack (the attacking firm aims at our strength) and the correct counter is to attack back in the firm's territory. Obviously this is a rarely used technique.

Offensive actions

New market segments: this uses behavioural segmentation (see the latter chapters on segmentation) and incentivizes consumer behaviour for a win-win relationship.

Go-to-market approaches: this learns about consumers' preferences in terms of bundling, channels, buying plans, etc.

Differentiating functionality: this approach extends consumers' needs by offering product and purchase combinations most compelling to potential customers.

Conclusion

The above was a brief introduction on both consumer behaviour and how that behaviour applies to marketing strategy. The over-arching point is that marketing science (and marketing research, marketing strategy, etc) should all be focused on consumer behaviour. Good marketing is consumer-centric. Have you heard that before?

Checklist

You'll be the smartest person in the room if you:

- [ ] Remember that in marketing, the consumer is central, NOT THE FIRM.

- [ ] Point out the consumer's problem is always how to maximize utilization/satisfaction while managing a limited budget.

- [ ] Think about the consumer's decision process while undertaking all analytic projects.

- [ ] Recall that strategy is a focus on consumer behaviour, not competitive behaviour.

- [ ] Remember that both Porter, and Treacy and Wiersema provide three general strategies.

- [ ] Observe that competitive combat can be thought of in terms of consumer behaviour.

What is an insight?

03

Introduction

An executive executes. An executive guides a company or a department by making decisions. An executive makes good decisions most of the time. Are these decisions based on facts? How do they know which lever to pull in order to alter the future course of key metrics?

The purpose of analytics is to provide insights. Good decisions are based on good insights. Right? But are insights used? How often? In fact, what is an insight?

Insights tend not to be used by executives

Executives do not typically use insights in decisions about running their companies or departments. *Information Week* (August 2005) reported that most managers in retail responsible for price setting prefer intuition to decisions based on analytics. Only about 5% reported using some kind of decision-support system. Rich, McCarthy and Harris (2009) found that about 40% of major decisions are not based on facts or insights but on the manager's intuition. Boston Consulting Group (Egan *et al*, 2009) found that less than 25% of executives managing at least a $1.5 billion company thought their analytic functions provided competitive advantage or positive ROI.

Here are a few quotes, collected from senior executives about insights they've received:

What they give me is not even relevant to my business.
CEO, $4 billion retailer

The results are usually too little, too late.
COO, $12 billion manufacturer

I get mostly tactics, not strategy.
VP Strategy, $2 billion insurance company

When I question the results, the next revision has drastic changes.
CMO, $22 billion hotel chain

Gives no actions, just describes problems.
CEO, $33 billion entertainment conglomerate

Most of the time I only see obvious, trivial output.
CMO, $2 billion casual dining business

If the above quotes are representative, generally speaking executives do not value very highly what are purported to be 'insights'. What they're given is not very useful, does not affect their business. The above seems to suggest that senior executives do not trust what they get from analysts. What they get from analysts is not very meaningful.

How can this be? Predictive analytics is entirely about THIS causes THAT. It might be that even analysts do not have a good definition for an insight.

Is this an insight?

Maybe even analysts do not know what an insight is. Perhaps what they produce is not of use to executives because they do not know what executives need. Below are statements I've heard, typically from consumer insights or advanced analytics groups, claiming to be insights, usually presented to senior marketing leaders:

- '92% of our customers wear some kind of jeans when they come to our store.'
- 'We have the highest-rated product in our industry.'

- 'Net revenue decreased over 3.5% YOY in same store sales.'
- 'Our customers trust our brand more than all other brands.'
- 'Both market research and independent field tests show treatment X outperforms treatment Y.'
- 'This trend is going up.'

The last 'insight' is particularly disturbing. It should be considered an observation and would not be defined as an insight. An insight is defined by a selection of interesting factors.

So, what is an insight?

Below is my attempt to formalize a definition of an insight.

An insight has to contain new information

The information has to be new, relevant and non-trivial. To be an insight, and not a mere observation, the information must be something more than 'This trend is going up'. It may even be counter-intuitive, which is often the most interesting finding.

More than once, in doing a model which has marketing communications (marcom) as independent variables, e-mail has been found to be negative. That is, as more e-mails are sent out, the amount of the dependent variable, say units or revenue, actually decreases. How can this be? E-mail fatigue is a common answer.

An insight must focus on understanding consumer behaviour

In marketing, the consumer is king. Consumer-centricity is the guiding concept in marketing. If the focus is on something else, it is probably not marketing. It may be finance or engineering or merchandising or operations or something else, but it is not marketing.

The whole point of marketing is an understanding and an incentivizing and a changing of consumer behaviour for a win to the consumer and a win to the firm. Going through the consumer's decision-making process is often valuable in this regard.

An insight has to quantify causality

An insight has to be about cause and effect. A marketer needs a lever to pull, something to DO to effect a change. An insight needs to measure how a change in one variable impacts a change in another variable.

For example, if a marketer was given the following model:

$$\text{Units} = f \text{ (seasonality, consumer confidence, corporate tax rates, industry growth and inflation)}$$

what can be done with it? What insights can come from it? What actions does it provide? Does the marketer have a lever to pull? NO! This model provides nothing actionable for the marketer and is therefore of limited use.

An insight has to provide a competitive advantage

An insight has to be a piece of intelligence the firm's competitors do not have. All intelligence is based on awareness of some information. An insight provides intelligence such that the firm is in a better competitive situation.

An insight must generate financial implications

An insight should be measurable. Whether an ROI or contribution margin or risk assessment, there should be some financial implications with any insight. If there is not a measured increase in revenue or satisfaction, or a measurable decrease in expenses, the validity of the analyses should be questioned.

Ultimately, an insight is about action-ability

All of the above drill down to one thing – action-ability. If an insight provides action-ability, within the dimensions mentioned, it is providing marketers with what they need to make better decisions. An executive must execute, must make decisions. The hypothesis is that if these decisions are based on data then the chance of making the right decision increases.

The job of the analyst is to provide insights. The comments above attempt to put structure around the defining of an insight, providing more than a mere observation, in the hopes that executives will actually USE the analyst's output and make better decisions.

Checklist

You'll be the smartest person in the room if you:

☐ Recognize the job of executives is to execute, that is, to make decisions. Decisions based on data tend to be better, more accurate, and less risky.

☐ Understand that executives tend NOT to use analytics because they do not trust analytics: most of what passes as analytic insights is too little and too late, very simple, very obvious.

☐ Decide on a new definition of what an insight is: an insight is more than a mere observation.

☐ Insist that to be an insight, it must:
   − contain new information;
   − focus on understanding consumer behaviour;
   − quantify causality;
   − provide a competitive advantage;
   − generate financial implications.

☐ Realize that ultimately a real analytic insight provides action-ability.

PART TWO
Dependent variable techniques

What drives demand?

04

Modelling dependent variable techniques

Introduction

Now, on to the first marketing problem: determining and quantifying those things that drive demand. Marketing is about consumer behaviour (which I've touched on but about which I will have more to say later) and the point of marketing is about incentivizing consumers to purchase. These purchases (typically units) are what economists call demand. (By the way, finance is more about supply and the two together are supply and demand. Remember back in Beginning Economics?)

Dependent equation type vs inter-relationship type statistics

Before we dive into the problem at hand, it might be good to back up and give some simple definitions. There are two kinds of (general) statistical techniques: the dependent equation type and the inter-relationship type. Dependent type statistics deal with explicit equations (which can either be deterministic or probabilistic, see below). Inter-relationship techniques are not equations, but the variance between variables. These will be covered/defined later but are types of factor analysis and segmentation. Clearly this current chapter is about an equation.

Deterministic vs probabilistic equations

Now let's talk about two kinds of equations: deterministic and probabilistic. Deterministic is algebraic ($y = mx + b$) and the left side exactly equals the right side.

$$Profit = Revenue - expenses.$$

If you know two of the quantities you can algebraically solve for the third. This is NOT the kind of equation dealt with in statistics. Of course not.

Statistics deals with probabilistic equations:

$$Y = a + bX_i + e.$$

Here Y is the dependent variable (say, sales, units or transactions), a is the constant or intercept, X is some independent variable(s) (say, price, advertising, seasonality), b is the coefficient or slope and e is the random error term. It's this random error term that makes this equation a probabilistic one. Y does not exactly $= a + bX_i$ because there is some random disturbance (e) that must be accounted for. Think of it as Y, on average, equals some intercept plus bX_i.

As an example, say Sales = constant + price * slope + error, that is, Sales = a + Price * b + e. Note that Y (sales) depends on price, +/–.

BUSINESS CASE

Okay, say we have a guy, Scott, who's an analytic manager at a PC manufacturing firm. Scott has an MS in economics and has been doing analytics for four years. He started mostly as an SAS programmer and has only recently been using statistical analysis to give insights to drive marketing science.

Scott is called into his boss's office. His boss is a good strategist with a direct marketing background but is not well versed in econometrics or analytics.

'Scott', the boss says, 'we need to find a way to predict our unit sales. More than that, we need something to help us understand what drives our unit sales. Something that we can use as a lever to help increase sales over the quarter.'

'A demand model.' Scott says. 'Units are a function of, what, price, advertising?'

'Sure.'

Scott gulps and says, 'I'll see what I can do.'

That night he thinks about it and has some ideas. He'll first have to think about causality ('Demand is caused by...') and then he'll have to get appropriate data.

It's smart to formulate a theoretic model first, regardless of what data you may or may not have. First, try to understand the data-generating process ('this is caused by that, and maybe that, etc') and then see what data, or proxies for data, can be used to actually construct the model.

It's also wise to hypothesize the signs of the (independent, right-hand side) variables you think significant in causing your dependent variable to vary. Remember that the dependent variable (left side of the equation) is dependent upon the independent variable(s) (right side of the equation).

For instance, it's well known that price is probably a significant variable in a unit-demand model and that the sign should be negative. That is, as price goes up, units, on average, should go down. This is the law of demand, the only law in all of economics – except the one that most economic forecasts will be wrong. ('Economists have predicted 12 of the last 7 recessions.')

(For you sticklers, yes, there is a 'Giffen good'. This is an odd product whereby an increasing price causes an increase in demand. These are usually non-normal goods (typically luxury goods) like fine art or wine. For the vast majority of products most marketers work on, however, these normal goods are ruled by the law of demand: price goes up, quantity (units) goes down.)

So Scott thinks that price and advertising spend are important in generating demand. Also that there should be something about the season. He's on the consumer side of the business and it has strong back-to-school and Christmas seasonal spikes.

He thinks he can easily get the number of units sold and the average price of those units. Seasonality is easy; it's just a variable to account for time of the year, say quarterly. Advertising spend (for the consumer market) might be a little tougher but let's say he is able to twist some arms and eventually secure a guess as to the average amount of advertising spend on the consumer market, by quarter.

This will be a time series model since it has season and quarterly units, average prices and advertising spend, by time period, quarterly. (There will be some econometric suggestions on time series modelling in the technical section, particularly pertaining to serial correlation.)

For now, let's make sure there's a good grasp of the problem. Scott will use a dependent variable technique called ordinary regression (ordinary least squares, OLS) to understand (quantify) how season, advertising spend and price cause (explain the movement of) units sold. This is called a structural analysis: he is trying to understand the structure of the data-generating process. He is attempting to quantify how price, advertising spend and season explain, or cause (most of) the movement in unit sales.

When he's through he'll be able to say whether or not advertising spend is significant in causing unit sales (he'll have to make certain no advertisers are in earshot when he does) and whether December is positive and January negative in terms of moving unit sales, etc.

Now, Scott is ready to design the ordinary regression model.

Conceptual notes

Ordinary regression is a common, well-understood and well-researched statistical technique that has been around for over 200 years. Remember that regression is a dependent variable technique, $Y = a + bX_i + e$, where e is a random error term not specifically seen but whose impact is felt in the distribution of the variables.

Ordinary regression: a statistical technique whereby a dependent variable depends on the movement of one or more independent variables (plus an error term).

Simple regression has one independent variable and multiple regression has more than one independent variable, that is:

$$y = a + b_1x_1 + b_2x_2...+ b_nx_n, \text{ etc}$$

Scott's model for his boss will use multiple regression because he has more than one independent variable.

The output of the model will have estimates about how significant each variable is (we'll see its coefficient or slope) and whether it's significant or not (based on its variance). This is the heart of structural analysis, quantifying the structure of the demand for PCs.

So, Scott collected data (see Table 4.1) and ran the model

$$\text{Units} = \text{price} + \text{advertising}$$

and now sees how the model fits.

There is one general measure of goodness of fit: R^2. R^2 is the square of the correlation coefficient, in this case the correlation of actual units and predicted units. While correlation measures strength and direction, R^2 measures shared variance (explanatory power) and ranges from 0% – 100%.

(An interesting but rather useless bit of trivia is why R^2 is called R^2. Yes, R^2 is the square of R, and R is the correlation coefficient. Correlation is symbolized as the Greek letter rho, ρ. Why? In Greek numerals $\alpha = 1$, $\beta = 2$, etc, and $\rho = 100$ (kind of like Roman numerals, $I = 1$, $II = 2$, $C = 100$, etc). Remember that the range of correlation is from –100% to +100%. ρ = rho and in English = R. Now impress your analytic friends.)

Table 4.1 Demand model data

Quarter	Unit sales	Avg price	Ad spend
1	50	1,400	6,250
2	52.5	1,250	6,565
3	55.7	1,199	6,999
4	62.3	1,099	7,799
1	52.5	1,299	6,555
2	59	1,200	7,333
3	58.2	1,211	7,266
..	..	..	..

Note the data is quarterly, which we'll address soon enough. Scott runs ordinary regression and finds the output as Table 4.2.

The first row is the estimated coefficient, or slope. Note that price is negative, as hypothesized. The second row is the standard error, or an estimate of the standard deviation of the variable, which is a measure of dispersion.

Table 4.2　Ordinary regression

	Ad spend	Avg price	Constant
Coefficient	0.0007	−0.0412	101.83
Stand err	0.0003	0.0047	
R^2	83%		
t-ratio	2.72	−8.67	

Standard error: an estimate of standard deviation, calculated as the standard deviation divided by the square root of the number of observations.

Let's talk about significance, shall we? In marketing we operate at 95% confidence. Remember z-scores? 1.96 is the z-score for 95% confidence, which is the same as a p-value < 0.05. So, if a t-ratio (which in this case is the coefficient divided by its standard error) is > |1.96| the variable is considered significant. Significance means that there's less than a 5% chance of the variable having 0 impact and the t-ratio tests for the probability that the variable's impact is likely to be 0.95% of all standard-normal observations will be within +/− 1.96 z-scores.

Notice that advertising spend has a coefficient of 0.0007 (rounded) and a standard error of 0.0003 (rounded). The t-ratio (coefficient divided by its standard error) is 2.72 which is > 1.96 so it is said to be positive and significant. ('Whew' the advertisers say.) Likewise price is significant (< −1.96) and negative, as expected.

Now let's mention fit; how well the model does with just these two variables. R^2 is the general measure of goodness of fit and in this case is 83%. That is, 83% of the variance between actual and predicted units is shared, or 83% of the movement of the actual dependent variable is 'explained' by the independent variables. This can be interpreted as 83% of the movement in the unit sales can be attributed to price and advertising spend. This seems pretty good; that's a fairly high amount of explanatory power. That's probably why Scott's boss wanted him to do this model.

The next step is for Scott to add seasonality, which he hypothesized to be a variable that impacts consumer PC units sold. Scott has quarterly data so this is easy to do. The new model will be units = price + advertising + season.

Let's talk about dummy variables (binary variables, those with only two values, 1 or 0). These are often called 'slope shifters' because their purpose (when turned 'on' as a 1) is to shift the slope coefficient up or down. The idea of a binary variable is to account for changes in two states of nature: on or off, yes or no, purchase or not, respond or not, q1 or not, etc.

Scott's model is a quarterly model so rather than use one variable called quarter with four values (1,2,3,4) he uses a model with three dummy (binary) variables, q2, q3 and q4, each 0 or 1. This allows him to quantify the impact of the quarter itself. Table 4.3 shows part of the dataset.

Table 4.3 Quarterly model

Quarter	Unit sales	Avg price	Ad spend	Q2	Q3	Q4
1	50	1,400	6,250	0	0	0
2	52.5	1,250	6,565	1	0	0
3	55.7	1,199	6,999	0	1	0
4	62.3	1,099	7,799	0	0	1
1	52.5	1,299	6,555	0	0	0
2	59	1,200	7,333	1	0	0
3	58.2	1,211	7,266	0	1	0
4	64.8	999	8,111	0	0	1
1	55	1,299	6,877	0	0	0
2	61.5	1,166	7,688	1	0	0
..	..	..	..	..	..	..

A brief technical note

When using binary variables that form a system, you cannot use them all. That is, for a quarterly model you have to drop one of the quarters. Otherwise the model won't solve (effectively trying to divide by 0) and you will have fallen into the 'dummy trap'. So Scott decides to drop q1, which means the interpretation of the coefficients on the quarters amounts to comparing each quarter to q1. That is, q1 is the baseline.

Now let's talk about the new model's (Table 4.4) output and diagnostics. Note first that R^2 improved to 95%, which means adding quarterly data improved the fit of the model. That is, price, advertising spend and season now explains 95% of the movement in unit sales, which is outstanding. It's a better model. Note the change in price and advertising coefficients.

Now, for what it means and how can it be used, the results of the output will be applied next.

Table 4.4   Regression output

	Q4	Q3	Q2	Ad spend	Avg price	Constant
Coefficient	3.825	2.689	1.533	0.0011	−0.0275	80.7153
Stand err	1.36	1.157	0.997	0.0003	0.0064	9.8496
R^2	95%					
t-ratio	2.81	2.32	1.54	4.1	−4.3	8.19

Results applied to business case

So now, what does all this tell us? Analytics without application to an actionable strategy is meaningless, much like special effects in a movie without a plot. Looking at the output again, Scott can make some actionable and important structural comments.

Again the R^2 as a measure of fit is > 95% which means the independent variables do a very good job explaining the movement of unit sales. All of the variables are significant at the 95% level (where z-score > $|1.96|$) except q2. The coefficients on the variables all have the expected signs. Comparing the quarters to q1 (which was dropped to avoid the dummy trap), Scott sees that they are all positive, which means they are all greater than q1, on average.

The powerful thing about ordinary regression is that it parcels out the impact of each independent variable, taking into account all the other variables. That is, it holds all other variables constant and quantifies the impact of each and every variable, one at a time. This means that, when taking all variables into account, q4 tends to add about 3.825 units more than q1. This is why a binary variable is called a slope shifter; just turning 'on' q4 adds 3.825 units, regardless what else is happening in price or advertising spend. Given the very strong seasonal pattern of unit sales these quarterly estimates seem reasonable.

Advertising has a significant and positive impact on unit sales. 0.0011 as a coefficient means every 1,000 increase in advertising spend tends to increase units by 1.1.

Now let's look at price. The price coefficient is negative, as expected at −0.0275. When price moves up by, say, 100, units tend to decrease by 2.75. Now, how can this be useful? Just knowing the quantification is valuable but more important is to calculate price elasticity.

Modelling elasticity

Elasticity is a microeconomic calculation that shows the per cent change in response given a per cent change in stimulus, or in this case, the per cent change in units sold given a per cent change in price.

> **Elasticity:** a metric with no scale or dimension, calculated as the per cent change in an output variable given a per cent change in an input variable.

Using a regression equation means the calculation of elasticity is: price coefficient * average price over average quantity (units).

$$\text{Elasticity} = \text{Bp } \bar{p}/\bar{q}$$

Average price is 1,102 and average quantity of units sold is 63 so the price elasticity calculated here is:

$$-0.0275 * 1,102 / 63 = -0.48$$

This means that if price increases by, say 10%, units sold will decrease by about 4.8%. This is strategically lucrative information allowing Scott and his team to optimize pricing to maximize units sold. There will be more on this topic later.

As a quick review, remember that there are two types of elasticity: elastic and inelastic.

> **Elastic demand:** a place on the demand curve where a change in an input variable produces more than that change in an output variable.

Inelasticity means that an X% increase in price causes a < X% decrease in units sold.

> **Inelastic demand:** a place on the demand curve where a change in an input variable produces less than that change in an output variable.

That is, if price were to increase by, say, 10%, units would decrease (remember the law of demand: if price goes up, quantity goes down) by less than 10%. Meaning, if elasticity < |1.00| the demand is inelastic (think of it as units being insensitive to a price change). If elasticity > |1.00| the demand is elastic.

The simple reason why elasticity is important to know is that it tells what happens to total revenue, in terms of pricing. In an inelastic demand curve total revenue follows price. So if price were to increase, total revenue would increase. See Table 4.5 below for a mathematical example.

Table 4.5   Elasticity, inelasticity, and total revenue

Inelastic	0.075		Increase price by	10.00%
p1	10.00	p2	11.00	10.00%
u1	1,000	u2	993	–0.75%
tr1	10,000	tr2	10,918	9.20%
Elastic	**1.25**		**Increase price by**	**10.00%**
p1	10.00	p2	11.00	10.00%
u1	1,000	u2	875	–12.50%
tr1	10,000	tr2	9,625	–3.80%

Let me add one quick note about elasticity modelling, something which is a common mistake. It is well known that if the natural logarithm is taken for all data (dependent as well as independent variables) then the elasticity calculation does not have to be done. Elasticity can be read right off the coefficient. That is, the beta coefficient IS the elasticity.

$$\ln(y) = b_1 \ln(x_1) + b_2 \ln(x_2) \ldots + b_n \ln(x_n)$$

The problem with this is that, while the calculation is easier (taking the price means and the unit means is not required), modelling all the data in natural logs specifically assumes a constant elasticity. This assumption seems heroic indeed. To say there is the same response to a 5% price change as there is to a 25% price change would strike most marketers as inappropriate. A model in logs would have a constantly concave curve to the origin throughout. For more on modelling elasticity from a marketing point of view, see an article I wrote that appeared in the *Canadian Journal of Marketing Research*, called 'Modeling elasticity' (Grigsby, 2002).

Using the model

How is the ordinary regression equation used? That is, how are predicted units calculated?

Note Figure 4.1 shows the actual as well as the predicted unit sales. The graph shows how well the predicted sales fit the actual sales. The equation is:

$$Y = a + b_1x_1 + b_2x_2 \ldots + b_nx_n \text{ or}$$

$$\text{Units} = \text{constant} + b_1*q2 + b_2*q3 + b_3*q4 + b_4*\text{price} + b_5*\text{advert}$$

Figure 4.1   Actual and predicted unit sales

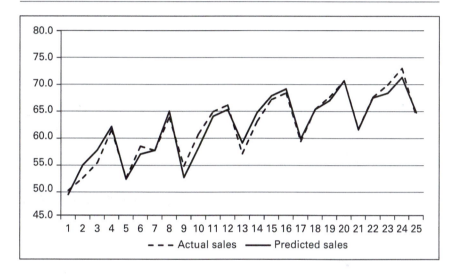

For the second observation (Table 4.6) this means:

$$80.7 + (3.8*0) + (2.6*0) + (1.533*1) + (0.0011*6,565)$$
$$- (0.0275*1,250) = 55.2$$

Table 4.6   Average price and ad spend

Quarter	Unit sales	Avg price	Ad spend	Q2	Q3	Q4	Predicted sales
1	50.0	1,400	6,250	0	0	0	49.2
2	52.5	1,250	6,565	1	0	0	55.2
3	55.7	1,199	6,999	0	1	0	58.2
4	62.3	1,099	7,799	0	0	1	63.0
1	52.5	1,299	6,555	0	0	0	52.3
2	59.0	1,200	7,333	1	0	0	57.5
3	58.2	1,211	7,266	0	1	0	58.2

Technical notes

We'll go over some detailed background information involving modelling in general and regression in particular now. This will be a little more technical and only necessary for a fuller understanding.

First, be aware that regression carries with it some 'baggage', some assumptions that if violated (and they/some almost always are to some extent) the model has shortcomings, bias, etc. As alluded to earlier, one of the best books on econometrics is Peter Kennedy's 1998 work *A Guide to Econometrics*. This is because he explains things first conceptually and then adds more technical/statistical detail, for those that want/need it. He covers the assumptions and failings of the assumptions of regression as well as anyone. My philosophy in this book is similar and this section will add some technical, but not necessarily mathematical, details.

The assumptions

The first assumption – dealing with functional form – is that the dependent variable (unit sales, above) can be modelled as a linear equation. This dependent variable 'depends' on the independent variables (season, price and advertising, as above) and some random error term.

The second assumption – dealing with the error term – is that the average value of the error term is zero.

The third assumption – dealing with the error term – is that the error term has similar variance scattered across all the independent variables (homoscedasticity) and that the error term in one period is not correlated with an error term in another (later) period (no serial (or auto) correlation).

The fourth assumption – dealing with independent variables – is that the independent variables are fixed in repeated samples.

The fifth assumption – dealing with independent variables – is that there is no exact correlation between the independent variables (no perfect collinearity).

Each of these assumptions is required for the regression model to work, to be interpretable, to be unbiased, efficient, consistent, etc. A failure of any of these assumptions means something has to be done to the model in order to account for the consequences of a violation of the assumption(s). That is, good model building requires a test for every assumption and, if the model fails the test, a correction to the model must be applied. All this requires an understanding of the consequences of violating every assumption.

All of these will be dealt with as we go through the business cases. But for now, let's just deal with serial correlation. Serial correlation means the error term in period x is correlated with the error term in period x + 1, all the way through the whole dataset. Serial correlation is very common in time series and must be dealt with.

A simple test, called the Durbin–Watson test, is easy to run in SAS to ascertain the extent of serial correlation. If the result of the test is about 2.00 there is not enough auto correlation to worry about.

The consequence of a violation of the assumption of no error term correlation is that the standard errors are biased downward, that is, the standard errors tend to be smaller than they should be. This means that the t-ratios (measures of significance) will be larger (appear more significant) than they really are. This is a problem.

The correction for serial correlation (at least for a 1-period correlation) is called Cochran–Orcutt (although the SAS output actually does a Yule–Walker estimate, which simply means it has ways to put the first observation back into the dataset) and it basically transforms all the data by the correlation of 1-period lag of the error term. The model is re-run and Durbin–Watson is re-run and those results used.

See Tables 4.7 and 4.8 for D–W being near 2.0 (from 1.08 to 1.93). This seems to indicate the model transformation worked. Note the change in coefficients: price went from –.0256 to –.0274. Note the standard error went from .006 to .004 and significance increased.

Table 4.7 Serial correlation

Variable	Estimate	Standard error	T value
Intercept	78.47	6.41	12.24
Price	–0.0256	0.006	–4.27
Advertising	0.001109	0.00019	5.65
Q2	1.5723	0.7422	2.12
Q3	2.9698	1.0038	2.96
Q4	4.357	0.8948	4.87
R^2	98.61%		
Durbin–Watson	1.08		

Table 4.8 Serial correlation

Variable	Estimate	Standard error	T value
Intercept	78.47	6.41	12.24
Price	−0.0274	0.004	−6.17
Advertising	0.001109	0.00019	5.65
Q2	1.5723	0.7422	2.12
Q3	2.9698	1.0038	2.96
Q4	4.357	0.8948	4.87
R^2	98.61%		
Durbin–Watson	1.93		

Now that the serial correlation has been taken care of, confidence in interpretation of the impacts of the model has improved. A quick note though about serial correlation and the diagnostics/corrections I've just mentioned. While most serial correlation is lagged on one period (called an autoregressive 1 or AR(1) process) this does not mean that there cannot be other serial correlation problems. Part of it is about the kind of data given. If it is daily data there will often be an AR(7) process. This means there is stronger correlation between periods lagged by 7 than periods lagged by 1. If there is monthly data there will often be an AR(12) process, etc. Thus, keep in mind the D–W stat is really only appropriate for an AR(1). That is, if the data is daily, each Monday would tend to be correlated with all other Mondays, etc. This means serial correlation of an AR(7) type, and not an AR(1). Thus, daily data tends to be lagged by 7 observations, monthly data tends to be lagged by 12 observations, quarterly data by 4, etc.

SEGMENTATION AND ELASTICITY MODELLING CAN MAXIMIZE REVENUE IN A RETAIL/MEDICAL CLINIC CHAIN: FIELD TEST RESULTS

Abstract

Most medical products or services are thought to be insensitive to price. This does not mean the best way to maximize revenue is to unilaterally raise every price indiscriminately for all regions in all clinics for all products or services. There should be some customers, some regions, some segments, some clinics, some products or services that are sensitive to price. Marketing analytics needs to give guidance to exploit these opportunities.

Using transactional and survey data from a large national retail/medical chain, I collected information that included, by customer and by clinic, the number of units, price paid and revenue realized for each product/service purchased over a two-year period. There was a telephone survey administered to contact three competing clinics around each of the firm's clinics and ascertain competitive prices charged for certain 'shopped' products/services. Thus, a dataset was created that had both own- and cross-price of several products or services.

Because much of a customer's purchasing behaviour could be attributed to clinic differences (staffing, employee courtesy, location, growth, operational discounts, etc), clinic segmentation was done. To emphasize, this was created to account for clinics influencing (causing) some customer behaviour other than responses to own- and cross-price. For example, one segment proved to be large (in terms of number of clinics), suburban and serving mostly loyal customers. Another segment was fairly small, urban and serving rather sick patients with customers who were mostly dissatisfied and had a high number of defectors. Obviously controlling for these differences was important.

After segmentation, elasticity modelling was done on each segment for selected products or services. This output showed that some segments and some products or services are sensitive to price; others are not. This details the ineffectiveness of simply raising prices on all products/services across the chain. In order to maximize revenue, prices should be lowered on a product in a clinic that is sensitive to price. This sensitivity comes from lack of loyalty, lack of long-term commitment, knowledge of competing prices, a customer's budget, etc.

After the analysis was finished and shown to the firm's management, they put a 90-day test vs control in place. They chose selected (shopped) products/segments and regions to test. After 90 days, the test clinics out-performed the control clinics, in terms of average net revenue, by > 10%. This seems to indicate that there are analytic ways to exploit price sensitivity in order to maximize revenue.

The problem and some background

Given a particular chain of retail/medical clinics across the nation, pricing practices were notoriously simplistic: raise prices on nearly every product or service, for every clinic, in every region, about the same amount, every year. Growth was achieved for a time but over the last handful of years customer satisfaction began to dip, defections increased, loyalty decreased, employee satisfaction/courtesy decreased, it was more and more difficult to operationally enforce price increases and the firm overall had minimal growth and larger and larger uses of discounts, etc. Much of the deterioration in these metrics was root-caused back to pricing policies. So the primary marketing problem was to understand to what extent pricing affected total revenue. That is, could price sensitivity be discovered differently by segment or region, for different products or services, to allow the firm to exploit those differences?

Pricing is mostly around one of two practices. The first, cost-plus, is a financial decision based on the input cost of the products or services and incorporating margin into the final price. This is the typical approach, especially in terms of products or services thought to be insensitive to price (eg, emergencies, radiology, major surgery, etc). The other pricing avenue is for shopped products or services. These are products or services thought to possibly be more sensitive to price (exams, discretionary vaccines, etc). For these products or services a survey was created and three competing clinics around each of the firm's clinics were called and asked what prices they charged. Then the firm typically increased their own prices (very much operationally as cost-plus) but with an understanding where the competition priced those same products or services. They sometimes listened to an individual clinic's request or protest for a less-than-typical price increase.

Description of the dataset

The transactional database provided own-firm behavioural data at the customer level. This could be rolled up to the clinic level. The transactional data included: products/services purchased, price paid for each, discount applied, total revenue, number of visits, time between visits, ailment/complaint, clinic visited, staffing, etc.

The clinic data included aggregations of the above, as well as trade area, location (rural vs urban), staffing and demographics from the census data mapped to zip code level. Also available was certain market research survey data. These included customer satisfaction/loyalty and defection surveys, employee satisfaction surveys, etc.

Most interesting was the competitive survey data. This survey asked three competitors near each of the firm's clinics what prices they charged for shopped products. Shopped products are those believed to be more price sensitive and included exams, vaccines, minor surgery, etc. Thus, for each of the firm's clinics, they looked at own prices paid by customers for every product/service (both shopped and other) as well as three competitors' prices charged for selected shopped products/services. The own-price data allowed elasticity modelling to be undertaken, and the cross-price data showed an interesting cause from competitive pressures. Sometimes these competitive pressures made a difference on own price sensitivity and sometimes not. This provided lucrative opportunities for marketing strategy.

First: segmentation

Why segment?

The first step was to do clinic segmentation.

> **Segmentation:** a marketing strategy aimed at dividing the market into sub-markets, wherein each member in each segment is very similar by some measure to each other and very dissimilar to members in all other segments.

This is because consumers' behaviour, in some ways, may be caused by a clinic's performance, staffing, culture, etc. That is, what might look like a consumer's choice might be caused more by a clinic's firmographics. The dataset contained all revenue and product transactions that could be rolled up by clinic. This meant that year-over-year growth, discounting changes, customer visits, etc, could be useful metrics. Also important was the location of a clinic (rural, urban, etc). So there was a lot of knowledge about the clinic and its performance and it was these things that it was necessary to control for in the elasticity models.

Because latent class analysis (LCA) has become the gold standard these last ten years, LCA was used as a segmentation technique. It has proven far superior to typical (k-means, a segmentation algorithm discussed later) techniques, especially in outputting maximally differentiated segments. An obvious point: the more differentiated segments are the more unique marketing strategies can be created for each segment.

Profile output

After running LCA on the clinic data, the profile below was created (see Table 4.9). A couple of comments on the segments, particularly those to be used in the field test. Segment 1 is the largest (in terms of number of clinics included) and has the largest per cent of annual revenue. Segment 1 is most heavily situated in suburban areas and market research shows them to have the most loyal customers. Segment 2 is the next-to-largest but only brings in about half of their fair share of revenue. Segment 4, while small, represents > 20% of overall revenue and is mostly in urban areas. Market research reveals this segment to be the least satisfied and contains the most defectors. These differences help account for customers' sensitivity to price, as will be shown in the models later.

Then: elasticity modelling

Overview of elasticity modelling

Let's go back to beginning microeconomics: price elasticity is the metric that measures the per cent change in an output variable (typically units) from a per cent change, in this case (net) price, from an input variable. If the per cent change is > 100%, that demand is called elastic. If it is < 100%, that demand is called inelastic. This is an unfortunate term. The clear concept is one of sensitivity. That is, how sensitive are customers who purchase units to a change in price? If there is a say 10% change in price and customers respond by purchasing < 10% units, they are clearly insensitive to price. If there is a say 10% change in price and customers respond by purchasing > 10% units, they are sensitive to price.

Table 4.9 Elasticity modelling

	Segment 1	Segment 2	Segment 4
% Market	36%	34%	7%
% Revenue	41%	19%	21%
# of clients	5,743	3,671	15,087
Rev/visit	135	120	215
% Suburb	56%	51%	45%
% Rural	13%	20%	3%
% Urban	31%	29%	52%

But this is not the key point, at least in terms of marketing strategy. The law of demand is that price and units are inversely correlated (remember the downward sloping demand curve?). Units will always go the opposite direction of a price change. But the real issue is what happens to revenue. Since revenue is price * units, if demand is inelastic, revenue will follow the price direction. If demand is elastic, revenue will follow the unit direction. Thus, to increase revenue in an inelastic demand curve, price should increase. To increase revenue in an elastic demand curve, price should decrease.

From point elasticity to modelling elasticity

Most of us were taught in microeconomics the simple idea of point elasticity. Point elasticity is the per cent difference between (x,y) points. That is, the per cent change in units given a per cent change in price. Say price goes from 9–11, and units go from 1000–850. The point elasticity is calculated as $[((1000-850) / 1000) / ((9-11) / 9)] = 0.15 / -0.22 = -0.675$ which is –68%. Note the per cent change in units is 15%, from a per cent change in price of 22%. Obviously units are a smaller change (less sensitive) than the price change so this (point) demand is inelastic. That is, the elasticity at this point on the demand curve is insensitive to price. Note that as the demand curve goes from a high price to a low price, the slope changes and the sensitivity changes. This is the key marketing strategy issue.

Thus elasticity is a marginal function over an average function. The overall mathematical concept of 'marginal' is the average slope of a curve which is a derivative. So to calculate the overall average elasticity requires the derivative of the units by price function (ie, the demand curve) measured at the means, meaning:

Elasticity = dQ/dP * average price / average units.

So mathematically the derivative represents the average slope of the demand function. In a statistical model (that accounts for random error) the same concept applies: a marginal function over an average function. In a statistical (regression) model the beta coefficient is the average slope, thus:

Elasticity = βPrice * average price / average units.

A quick note on a mathematically correct but practically incorrect concept: modelling elasticity in logs. While it's true that if the natural log is taken both of the demand and price, there is no calculation at the means; the beta coefficient is the elasticity. However – and this is important – running a model in natural logs also implies a very wrong assumption: constant elasticity. This means there is the same impact at a small price change as at a large price change and no marketer believes that. Thus, modelling in natural logs is never recommended.

Own-price vs cross-price and substitutes

Now comes the interesting part of this dataset. It has competitor prices! A survey was done asking three competitors nearest to each clinic the prices they charged for 'shopped products'. These products are assumed to be generally price sensitive. I took the highest competitor price and the lowest competitor price and used that as cross-price data for every (shopped) product. Thus the demand model (by segment) for each shopped product will be:

Units = f(own-price, high cross-price, low cross-price, etc)

The reason competitive prices are so interesting is because of two things. First, competitive prices are causes of behaviour. Second, if a competitor is a strong substitute, strategic choices reveal themselves.

A competitor is regarded as a substitute if the coefficient on their cross-price is positive. This means there is a positive correlation with a firm's own demand. Thus, if the competition is a substitute and chooses to raise their prices, our own demand will increase because their customers will tend to flow to our demand (with lower prices). If the competitor is a substitute and chooses to lower their prices, our own demand will decrease because their customers will tend to flow out of our demand (with higher prices). Thus, knowing if a competitor is a substitute gives explanatory power to the model as well as a potential strategic lever.

But the real issue is how strong a substitute a competitor is. This strength is revealed in the cross-price coefficients. Say for a particular demand model the coefficient on own price is –1.50 and the coefficient on high cross-price is +1.10. Own price has the expected negative correlation (own price goes up, (own) units go down). High cross-price is positive, meaning in this case the high-price competitor is a substitute. If own elasticity is price sensitive and we lower our prices, the high competitors can lower their prices as well, decreasing our demand. But note that they are not a strong substitute. A strong substitute will not only have a positive coefficient but that coefficient will be (absolute value) > own price coefficient. Meaning, in the above example, if we lower our prices by 10% we expect our demand to increase by 15%. If the competitor matches our price change and lowers by 10%, that will affect our demand by 11%, that is, they were not a strong substitute.

However, if our own price coefficient was –1.50 and the high-price competitor coefficient was instead +3.00, a very different story unfolds. If we lower our prices by 10% our demand will go up by 15%. But the strong substitute can lower their price by 5% and impact our units by 15% (5% * 3 = 1.5). Or if they also lower by 10% and match us that will impact our units by 30%! Clearly this strong competitor is far more powerful than the first scenario. Note also that none of this 'game theory' knowledge is possible without cross-prices.

Modelling output by segment

The next four tables show *elasticity modelling* results by segment by four selected shopped products. (In the field test only vaccines (two), minor surgery and exams were used.) Following each table are notes on strategic uses.

Table 4.10 Elasticity modelling

Vaccine x	Seg 1	Seg 2	Seg 4
Vaccine x firm	–0.377	–1.842	–3.702
Vaccine x comp hi	–0.839	0.062	1.326
Vaccine x comp lo	–0.078	–0.167	–0.757

Segment 1: An elasticity < |1.00| (0.377, in absolute terms) means this product for this segment has a demand that is inelastic. This segment is loyal (via market research) and no competitor is a substitute (no positive cross-price elasticity). Therefore increase price.

A few details on segment 1 vaccine x calculations follow. For own-price elasticity, the firm's price was 28 and the own price coefficient was –1.2 and the average units were 89. Thus own price elasticity is –0.377 = –1.2 * 28/89. High competitor price elasticity is calculated as –0.839 = –1.915 * 39/89 and low price competitor elasticity is –0.078 = –0.33 * 21/89. All other calculations are similar.

Segment 2: An elasticity > |1.00| (1.842, in absolute terms) means this product for this segment has a demand that is elastic. The high competitor is a weak substitute (0.062). Therefore decrease price.

Segment 4: An elasticity > 1.00 (3.702, in absolute terms) means this product for this segment has a demand that is elastic. This segment tends to be dissatisfied with a high number of defectors (via market research). The high competitor is a weak substitute (1.326). Therefore decrease price.

Table 4.11   Further elasticity modelling

Vaccine y	Seg 1	Seg 2	Seg 4
Vaccine y firm	–0.214	–0.361	–0.406
Vaccine y comp hi	0.275	0.018	0.109
Vaccine y comp lo	0.196	0.123	0.864

Segment 1: An elasticity < |1.00| (0.214, in absolute terms) means this product for this segment has a demand that is inelastic. This segment is loyal (via market research) and the low competitor is a weak substitute. The high competitor is a strong substitute. Note the positive 0.275 is > absolute 0.214 meaning the high competitor can match/retaliate against the firm with a smaller price decrease. Therefore test (remember this segment is loyal) increasing price.

Segment 2: An elasticity < |1.00| (0.361, in absolute terms) means this product for this segment has a demand that is inelastic. While both competitors are substitutes, they each are weak. Therefore test increasing price.

Segment 4: An elasticity < |1.00| (0.406, in absolute terms) means this product for this segment has a demand that is (surprisingly) inelastic. This segment tends to be dissatisfied with a high number of defectors (via market research). While both competitors are substitutes, the low competitor is a strong substitute. Therefore cautiously test increasing price.

Table 4.12 Further elasticity modelling

Minor surgery	Seg 1	Seg 2	Seg 4
Min surg firm	−0.573	−0.173	−1.09
Min surg comp hi	0.202	0.475	−0.59
Min surg comp lo	−0.06	0.291	0.215

Segment 1: An elasticity < |1.00| (0.573, in absolute terms) means this product for this segment has a demand that is inelastic. This segment is loyal (via market research) and the high competitor is a weak substitute. Therefore test increasing price.

Segment 2: An elasticity < |1.00| (0.173, in absolute terms) means this product for this segment has a demand that is inelastic. Both competitors are strong substitutes. Therefore (cautiously) test increasing price.

Segment 4: An elasticity > |1.00| (1.090, in absolute terms) means this product for this segment has a demand that is (barely) elastic. This segment tends to be dissatisfied with a high number of defectors (via market research). The low competitor is a weak substitute. Therefore test decreasing price.

Table 4.13 Further elasticity modelling

Exams	Seg 1	Seg 2	Seg 4
Exam firm	−0.1	−0.025	−0.1
Exam comp hi	0.008	0.075	0.095
Exam comp lo	−0.02	−0.03	0.023

Segment 1: An elasticity < |1.00| (0.100, in absolute terms) means this product for this segment has a demand that is inelastic. This segment is loyal (via market research) and the high competitor is a weak substitute. Therefore test increasing price.

Segment 2: An elasticity < |1.00| (0.025, in absolute terms) means this product for this segment has a demand that is inelastic. The high competitor is a strong substitute. Therefore test increasing price.

Segment 4: An elasticity < |1.00| (0.095, in absolute terms) means this product for this segment has a demand that is inelastic. This segment tends to be dissatisfied with a high number of defectors (via market research). Both competitors are substitutes and the high competitor is a strong substitute. Therefore (cautiously) test increasing price.

The above analysis shows how elasticity can be used as a strategic weapon. Because it involves both own-price (customers' sensitivity) as well as cross-price (potential competitor's retaliation) the strategic levers are lucrative.

Example of elasticity guidance

Now let's talk about transferring the modelling from the segment level to the clinic level, where pricing guidance needs to be. The basic idea was to use the segment model's price coefficient and apply that to the elasticity calculation by clinic. That is, elasticity at the segment level:

Segment quantity =
Segment price-coefficient * segment average price/segment average quantity.

Translating elasticity to (each) clinic:

Clinic quantity =
Segment price-coefficient * clinic average price/clinic average quantity.

Now let's look at a particular clinic's test results. This clinic is in segment 4, a very price sensitive segment. Guidance for vaccine x (at this clinic) was to decrease price by 6%. This decrease brought the clinic's price position down from the highest (compared to the surrounding competitors) to a middle-priced option. The high competitor was a weak substitute, so strong retaliation was thought unlikely.

For the vaccine x product, during the 90-day field test, this clinic generated 2,292 in vaccine x revenue and sold 84 units, making average net revenue of 27.28. The matched control cell was 25.86, giving a 5.48% test-over-control result. This comes from two things interacting: first, this segment in general is sensitive to price and second, this clinic has no (strong) substitutes. Thus guidance was to decrease price with no fear of retaliation from the competitors.

Look at another particular clinic's test results. This clinic is in segment 1, a price insensitive segment. Guidance for exams (at this clinic) was to increase price by 2%. This increase brought the clinic's price position up from the middle (compared to the surrounding competitors) to the highest-priced option. Remember this segment tends to be very loyal. The high competitor was a weak substitute, so strong retaliation was thought unlikely.

For the exam product, during the 90-day field test, this clinic generated 27,882 in exam revenue and sold 499 units making average net revenue of 55.88. The matched control cell was 47.41 giving a 17.85% test-over-control result. This comes from two things interacting: first, this segment in general is insensitive to price and second, this segment and this clinic have no (strong) substitutes. Thus guidance was to increase price with no fear of retaliation from either the customers or competitors.

Last: test vs control

There were nearly 100 clinics that met criteria to be part of the field test. There were about 25 test clinics and 75 control clinics. The test clinics would get the elasticity guidance and the control clinics would continue business as usual.

Matched cells by region by segment were designed. The test metric was average net revenue (by region, by segment, by product, etc). The overall result was that the test clinics out-performed the control clinics, in terms of average net revenue, by > 10% in 90 days. Of course regions and segments and products had a distribution of results. One region was extremely positive, another region was slightly negative, one segment (segment 1, the loyal segment) was very positive and segment 4 (the dissatisfied segment) was less so. Such a strong overall result indicates elasticity analysis can help guide optimal pricing.

Discussion

Is there game theory in the medical services world? Most practitioners would probably say not really, their job is more about patient care than competition. However, one interesting example that might contradict common wisdom comes from this study.

There happened to be two clinics, call them X and Y, which each came from the same region, the same segment 4, but one had a strong substitute (low) competitor and the other did not. For exams, both clinics were given a price decrease of 4%. The clinic that faced the strong competitor (clinic X) had one half the average net revenue gains vs control as clinic Y. This might indicate the low competitor around clinic X also lowered their exam prices (next survey will verify) but because they were a strong substitute they only needed to lower by 1% to negatively impact the firm's 4% price decrease.

It seems that at least for the shopped products, prices in the medical services area are NOT so insensitive. It also seems that some kind of 'game theory' might go on, especially in close locale, to respond and retaliate with price changes. That was probably why the competitive survey was done in the first place.

Conclusion

Why is elasticity modelling so rarely done?

In my nearly 30 years of marketing analysis over a wide variety of firms in many different industries, elasticity modelling (as discussed here) is virtually never done. Often there are surveys on prices and purchasing, etc. But this is self-reported and probably self-serving ('Yes, your prices are too high!'). Another common and slightly better marketing research technique is conjoint analysis. It is somewhat artificial and still self-reported but analytically controls for such things.

My point is that if there is real behaviour – real purchasing responses based on real price changes – in the transactional database, why would THOSE data elements not be best to measure price sensitivity? The answer seems to be that translating what was learned in microeconomics into statistical analysis is a wide step and not usually taught. That is, going from point elasticity to statistically modelling elasticity is knowledge not easily gained. Note, however, the steps are quite straightforward and the modelling is not difficult. Perhaps this chapter is one way to get elasticity modelling used more in practice, especially given the potential benefits.

Checklist

You'll be the smartest person in the room if you:

☐ Remember there are two types of statistical analysis: dependent variable types and inter-relationship types.

☐ Recall that there are two types of equations: deterministic and probabilistic.

☐ Observe that regression (ordinary least squares, OLS) is a dependent variable type analysis using independent variables to explain the movement in a dependent variable.

☐ Point out that R^2 is a measure of goodness of fit; it shows both explanatory power and shared variance between the actual dependent variable and the predicted dependent variable.

☐ Remember that the t-ratio is an indication of statistical significance.

☐ Always avoid the 'dummy trap'; keep one less binary variable in a system (eg, in a quarterly model only use three not four quarters).

☐ Think in terms of the two kinds of elasticity: inelastic and elastic demand curves.

☐ Focus on the real issue of elasticity: what impact it has on total revenue (not units).

☐ Remember price and units are negatively correlated. In an inelastic demand curve total revenue follows price; in an elastic demand curve total revenue follows units. To increase total revenue in an inelastic demand curve price should increase; to increase total revenue in an elastic demand curve price should decrease.

☐ Remember that regression comes with assumptions.

Who is most likely to buy and how do I target them?

Introduction

The next marketing question is around targeting, particularly who is likely to buy. Note that this question is statistically the same as 'Who is likely to respond (to a message, an offer, etc)?' This probability question is the centre of marketing science in that it involves understanding choice behaviour. The typical technique involved (especially for database/direct marketing) is logistic regression.

Conceptual notes

Logistic regression has a lot of similarities to ordinary regression. They both have a dependent variable, they both have independent variables, they are both single equations, and they both have diagnostics around the impact of independent variables on the dependent variable as well as 'fit' diagnostics.

But their differences are also many. Logistic regression has a dependent variable that takes on only two (as opposed to continuous) values: 0 or 1, that is, it's binary. Logistic regression does not use the criteria of 'minimizing the sum of the squared errors' (which is ordinary least squares, or OLS) to calculate the coefficients, but rather maximum likelihood via a grid search. The interpretation of the coefficients is different. Odds ratios (e^{β}) are typically used and fit is not about a predicted vs an actual dependent variable.

> **Maximum likelihood:** an estimation technique (as opposed to ordinary least squares) that finds estimators that maximize the likelihood function observing the sample given.

As a slight detail, another important difference between logistic regression and ordinary regression is that logistic regression actually models the 'logit' rather than the dependent variable. A logit is the log of the event/ (1 – the event), that is, the log of the odds of the event occurring. Recall that ordinary regression models the dependent variable itself.

(By the way, yes there is a technique that can model > two values, but not continuous. That is, the dependent variable might have 3 or 4 or 5, etc, values. This technique is called multinomial logit (discriminate analysis will do this as well) but we will not cover it except to say it's the same as logistic regression, but the dependent variable has codes for multiple different values, rather than only 0 or 1.) All of the above means that the output of logistic regression is a probability between 0% and 100%, whereas the output of ordinary regression is an estimated (predicted) value to fit the actual dependent variable. Figure 5.1 shows a plot of actual events (the 0s and the 1s) as well as the logistic (s-curve).

Now let's look at some data and run a model, because that's where all the fun is.

Figure 5.1   Actual events and logistics

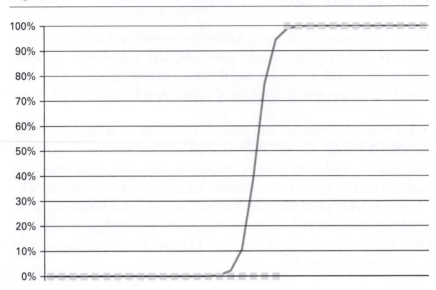

BUSINESS CASE

Now Scott's boss, very impressed with what he did on demand modelling, calls Scott into his office.

'Scott, we need to better target those likely to buy our products. We send out millions of catalogues, based on magazine subscriber lists, but the response rate is too small. What can we do to make our mailing ROI better?'

Scott thinks for a minute. The response rate was too small? Response rate is the rate of response, which is the number of those that responded (purchased), divided by the total number that got the communication. It's an overall metric of success.

'We want to target those likely to purchase based on a collection of characteristics. We have both customers and non-customers in our database – from the subscriber lists we've been mailing – so we could model the probability to respond based on clone or lookalike modelling.'

'What does that mean?' the boss asks.

'I'll have to dig into it a bit more but I know we can develop a regression-type model that scores the database with different probabilities to purchase for each name. We can sort the database by probability to purchase and only mail as deep as ROI limits.'

'Sounds good. Get to work on that and let me know when you have something.' With that the boss swivels in his chair so Scott knows the conversation is over.

Results applied to the model

Note Table 5.1 below, which shows the simplified dataset. This is a list of customers that purchased and those that did not purchase. Scott has data on which campaigns they each received, as well as some demographics. The objective is to figure out which of the non-purchasers 'look like' those that did purchase and re-mail them, perhaps with the same campaign (if we find one that was effective) or design another campaign.

The end result will be to score the database with 'probability to purchase' in order to understand what (statistically) works and strategize what to do next time. This is the cornerstone of direct (database) marketing.

Using the (contrived) dataset, you can run proc logistic descending in SAS. See Table 5.2 for the output of the coefficients. These coefficients are not interpreted the same way as in ordinary regression.

Because logistic regression is curvilinear and bound by 0 and 1, the impact of the independent variables affects the dependent variable differently. The actual impact is

$$e \text{ ^ coefficient}$$

For example, education's coefficient is 0.200. The impact would be:

$$e^{.200} = 1.225, \text{ that is } (2.71828 \text{ ^ } .200)$$

This means that for every year of added education, the increase in probability is 22.5%. This metric is called the odds ratio. This obviously has targeting implications: aim our product at the highest educated families as possible. Note that two of the three campaigns are negative (which tend to decrease probability to purchase) so this also adds credence to needing better targeting.

For logistic regression, there is not really a goodness of fit measure, like R^2 in OLS. Logit has a probability output between a dependent variable of 1 and 0. Often the 'confusion matrix' is used, and predictive accuracy is a sign of a good model. Table 5.3 shows the confusion matrix of the above model. (The confusion matrix from SAS uses 'ctable' as an option.) Say there are 10,000 observations.

The total number of events (purchases) is 6,750 + 1,750 or 8,500. The model predicted only 6,750 + 500 or 7,250. The total accuracy of the model is the actual events predicted correctly and the actual non-events predicted correctly, meaning 6,750 + 1,000 or 7,750/10,000 = 77.5%. The number of false positives is 500 (the model predicted 500 people would have the event that did not). This is an important measure of direct marketing, in terms of the cost of a wrong mailing.

Table 5.1 Simplified dataset

Id	Revenue	Purchase	Campaign a	Campaign b	Campaign c	Income	Size hh	Educ
999	1500	1	1	0	1	150000	1	19
1001	1400	1	1	0	1	137500	1	19
1003	1250	1	1	0	0	125000	2	15
1005	1100	1	1	0	0	112500	2	13
1007	2100	1	0	1	0	145000	3	16
1009	849	1	0	0	0	132500	3	17
1010	750	1	0	0	0	165000	3	16
1011	700	1	0	0	0	152500	3	9
1013	550	1	1	0	1	140000	4	15
1015	850	1	1	0	1	127500	4	18
1017	450	1	1	0	1	115000	4	17
1019	0	0	0	0	1	102500	5	16
1021	0	0	0	0	1	99000	6	15
1023	0	0	0	1	1	86500	7	16
1025	0	0	0	1	1	74000	6	15
1027	0	0	0	1	1	61500	5	14
1029	0	0	0	1	1	49000	4	13
1033	0	0	1	0	1	111000	4	12
1034	0	0	0	0	1	98500	3	11
1035	0	0	0	0	1	86000	3	10

Table 5.2 Co-efficient output

Intercept	-57.9
Campaign a	-8.48
Campaign b	16.52
Campaign c	-9.96
Income	0.001
Size hh	-3.41
Education	0.2

Table 5.3 Confusion matrix

	Actual non-events	**Actual events**
Predicted non-events	1,000	1,750
Predicted events	500	6,750

As an analytic 'trick' it often helps to determine if the dependent variable (sales, in this case) has any abnormal observations. Remember the z-score? This is a fast and simple way to check if an observation is 'out of bounds'. The z-score is calculated as ((observation – mean) / standard deviation).

Let's say the mean of revenue is 358.45 and the standard deviation of revenue is 569.72. So, if you run this calculation for all the observations on revenue you will see that (Table 5.1) id # 1007 ((2,100 – 358.45) / 569.72) = 3.057. This means that observation is > 3 standard deviations from the mean, a very non-normal observation. It is common to add a new variable, call it 'positive outlier' and it will take the values of 0 as long as the z-score on sales is < 3.00, then it takes the value of 1 if z-score > 3. Use this new variable as another independent variable to help account for outliers. Some of the coefficients should change and the fit usually improves. This new variable can be seen as an influential observation.

Note the slight changes in coefficients (Table 5.4). This ought to mean predictive accuracy increases. Note the updated confusion matrix below (Table 5.5).

The total number of events (purchases) is still **8,500** but note the shift in accuracy. The model now predicts 7,500 + 250 = 7,750. The total accuracy of the model is the actual events predicted correctly and the actual non-events predicted

Table 5.4   New variables

Intercept	−51.9
Influence	15.54
Campaign a	−6.06
Campaign b	16.6
Campaign c	−9.07
Income	0.002
Size hh	−1.65
Education	0.211

Table 5.5   Updated confusion matrix

	Actual non-events	**Actual events**
Predicted non-events	1,250	1,000
Predicted events	250	7,500

correctly, meaning 7,500 + 1,250 or 8,750/10,000 = 87.5%. The number of false positives is 250 (the model predicted 250 people would have the event that did not). This is an important measure of direct marketing, in terms of the cost of a wrong mailing. The model improved because of accounting for influential observations.

Lift charts

A common and important tool, especially in direct/database marketing is the lift (or gains) chart.

> **Lift/gains chart**: a visual device to aid in interpreting how a model performs. It compares by deciles the model's predictive power to random.

This is a simple analytic device to ascertain general fit as well as a targeting aid in terms of how deep to mail.

The general procedure is to run the model and output the probability to respond. Sort the database by probability to respond and divide into 10 equal 'buckets'. Then count the number of actual responders in each decile. If the model is a good one, there will be a lot more responders in the upper deciles and a lot fewer responders in the lower deciles.

As an example, say the average response rate is 5%. We have 10,000 total observations (customers). Each decile has 1,000 customers in it, some of them have responded and some of them have not. Overall there are 500 responders (500/10,000 = 5%). So, randomly, we would expect on average 50 in each decile. Instead, because the model works, say there are 250 in decile 1 and it decreases until the bottom decile has only one responder in it. The 'lift' is defined as the number of responders in each decile divided by the average (expected) number of responders. In decile 1 this means 250/50 = 500%. This shows us that the first decile has a lift of 5X, that there are five times more responders there than average. It also says that those in the top decile who did not respond are very good targets, since again, they all 'look alike'. This is an indication the model can discriminate the responders from the non-responders.

Figure 5.2   Lift chart

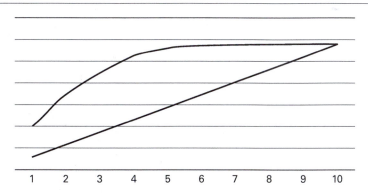

Note that in each decile there are 1,000 customers. 250 already responded in decile 1. All of the customers in decile 1 have a high probability of top 10% responding. There are 750 more potential targets in decile 1 that have NOT responded. This is the place to focus targeting and this is why it's called 'clone modelling'.

To briefly address the database marketing question, 'How deep do I mail?' let's look at the lift chart above (Figure 5.2). This is an accumulation of actual responders compared to expected responders. Depending on budget, etc, this lift chart helps to target. Most database marketers will mail as far as any decile out-responds the average. That is, until the lift is < 100%. Another way of saying this is to mail until the maximum distance between the curves is achieved. However, as a practical matter, most direct marketers (especially cataloguers) have a set budget and can only AFFORD to mail so deep, regardless of the statistical performance of the model. Thus, most of the attention is on the first one or two deciles.

Using the model – collinearity overview

Another very common issue that must be dealt with in (especially) regression modelling is collinearity.

Collinearity: a measure of how variables are correlated with each other.

Collinearity is defined as one or more independent variables that are more correlated with each other than either of them is with the dependent variable. That is, if there are, say two independent variables in the model, damaging collinearity is if X_1 and X_2 are more correlated than X_1 and Y and/or X_2 and Y. Mathematically:

$$\rho(X_1,X_2) > \rho(Y,X_1) \text{ or } \rho(Y,X_2) \text{ where } \rho = \text{correlation.}$$

The consequences of collinearity are that, while the parameter estimates of each independent variable remain unbiased, the standard errors are too wide. This means when significance testing is calculated (parameter estimate/standard error of the estimate) for a t-ratio (or a Wald ratio) these variables tend to show less significance than they really have. This is because the standard error is too large. Collinearity can also switch signs which return nonsensical results. Thus, collinearity must be tested and dealt with.

A quick note on overly simplistic 'diagnostics' I've seen in practice follows. It's possible to run a correlation matrix on the variables and obtain the (simple Pearson) correlation coefficient for each pair. This does

NOT check for damaging collinearity, this is a check for simple (linear) correlation. I've seen analysts just run the matrix and drop (yes, drop!) an independent variable just because the correlation of it and another independent variable is, say, greater than 80%. (Where did they get 80%? This is arbitrary and beneath anyone calling themselves analytic.) Okay, off the soap box.

The above 'testing' is irksome because real testing (with SAS and SPSS) is relatively easy. VIF is the most common. Run proc regress and include '/VIF' as an option. VIF is the variance inflation factor. Basically it regresses each independent variable on all other independent variables and displays a metric. This metric is $1/(1 - R^2)$. If this metric is > 10.0 (indicating an R^2 of > 90%) then as a rule of thumb, some variable is too collinear to ignore. That is, if there are three independent variables in the model, x_1, x_2 and x_3, VIF will regress $x_1 = f(x_2$ and $x_3)$ and show R^2, then $x_2 = f(x_1$ and $x_3)$ and show R^2 and last $x_3 = f(x_1$ and $x_2)$ and show R^2.

Note that we are not really testing for collinearity (because there will nearly ALWAYS be some collinearity). We are testing for collinearity bad enough to cause a problem (called ill conditioning).

The recommended approach is to include variables that make theoretic sense. If VIF indicates a variable is causing a problem but there is a strong reason for that variable to be included, one of the other variables should be examined instead. (It is important to note that dropping a variable is NOT the first course of action. Simply dropping a variable is arbitrary (and very simplistic) analytics. That is, a stronger, more defendable model results from a strategic understanding of the data generating process, not based on statistical diagnostics. The science of modelling would emphasize diagnostics; the art of modelling would emphasize balance and business impact. Did I mention sometimes in a practical business environment 'bad statistics' are allowed balanced on running a business? Gasp!

Depending on the issues and data, etc, other possible solutions exist. Putting all the independent variables in a factor matrix would keep the variables' variance intact but the factors are, by definition, orthogonal (uncorrelated).

Another (correcting) technique is called ridge regression (typically using Stein estimates) and requires special software (in SAS 'proc reg data = x.x outvif outset = xx ridge = 0 to 1 by 0.01; model y = x1 x2', etc) and expertise to use. In general, it trades collinearity for bias in the parameter estimates. Again, the balance is in knowing the coefficients are now biased but a drastic reduction in collinearity results. Is it worth it? Sorry, but the answer is, it depends.

While VIF is helpful, the condition index has become (since Belsley, Kuh and Welsch's 1980 book *Regression Diagnostics*) the state of the art in collinearity diagnostics. The maths behind it is fascinating but many text books will illuminate that. We will focus on an example. The approach, without getting TOO mathematical, is to calculate the condition index of each variable. The condition index is the square root of the largest eigenvalue (called the characteristic root) divided by each variable's eigenvalue. (An eigenvalue is the variance of each principal component when used in the correlation matrix.) The eigenvalues add up to the number of variables (including the intercept): see Table 5.6 below. This is a powerful diagnostic because a set of eigenvalues of relatively equal magnitude indicates that there is little collinearity. A small number of large eigenvalues indicates that a small number of component variables describe most of the variability of the variables. A zero eigenvalue implies perfect collinearity and – this is important – very small eigenvalues mean there is severe collinearity. Again, an eigenvalue near 0.00 indicates collinearity. As a rule of thumb, a condition index > 30 indicates severe collinearity.

Common outputs along with the VIF and condition index are the proportions of variance (see Table 5.6). This proportion of variance shows the percentage of the variance of the coefficient associated with each eigenvalue. A high proportion of variance reveals a strong association with the eigenvalue.

Let's talk about Table 5.6. First look at the condition index. The eigenvalue on the intercept is 6.86 and the first condition index is the square root of 6.86/6.86 = 1.00. Now the second condition index is the square root of 6.86/0.082 = 9.142. The diagnostics indicate that there are as many collinearity problems as there are condition indexes > 30, or in this case there may be three problems (230.42, 1048.1 and 432750). Look to the proportion of variance table. Any proportion > 0.50 is a red flag. Look at the last X6 variable. Variable X6 is related to the intercept, X1, X4 and X5. X5 is related to X2 (0.8306) and X6 (0.504). This indicates X6 is the most problematic variable. Something ought to be done about that.

Possible solutions might mean combining X5 and X6 into a factor and use the resulting factor as a variable instead of X5 and X6 as currently measured. This is because factors are by construction uncorrelated (we call it orthogonal). Another option would be to transform (especially) X6, either taking its exponent, or square root, or something else. The point is to try to find an X6-like variable correlated with the dependent variable

Table 5.6 Variance

Ind var	Eigenvalue	Cond index	Prop inter	Prop X1	Prop X2	Prop X3	Prop X4	Prop X5	Prop X6
X1	6.861	1.000	0.000	0.000	0.000	0.000	0.000	0.000	0.000
X2	0.082	9.142	0.000	0.000	0.000	0.091	0.014	0.000	0.000
X3	0.046	12.256	0.000	0.000	0.000	0.064	0.001	0.000	0.000
X4	0.011	25.337	0.000	0.000	0.000	0.427	0.065	0.001	0.000
X5	0.000	230.420	0.000	0.000	0.000	0.115	0.006	0.016	0.456
X6	0.000	1048.100	0.000	0.000	0.831	0.000	0.225	0.328	0.504
X7	0.000	432750.000	0.999	1.000	0.160	0.320	0.689	0.655	0.038

but LESS CORRELATED with, especially, X5. Are you able to get a larger sample? Can you take differences in X6, rather than just the raw measure? And yes, if there is a theoretical reason, you can drop X6 and re-run the model and see what you have. Dropping a variable is a last resort. Have I mentioned that?

A brief procedural note

On probably most of the analytic techniques we'll talk about, certain assumptions are built in. That is, regression has many assumptions about linearity, normality, etc. While for OLS I mentioned one assumption (especially for time series data) was no serial correlation, this same assumption is applied to logistic regression as well. Most regression techniques use most of these assumptions. So while in logit I showed how to test and correct for collinearity, this same test needs to be applied in OLS as well. It just happened to come up during our discussion of logistic regression.

This means that in reality, for every regression technique used, every assumption should be checked and every violation of assumptions should be tested for and corrected, if possible. This goes for OLS, logit and anything else. Okay?

Variable diagnostics

As in all regression, a significance test is performed on the independent variables but because logit is non-linear, the t-test becomes the Wald test (which is the t-test squared, so $1.96^2 = 3.84$, at 95%). The p-value still needs to be < 0.05.

Pseudo R^2

Logistic regression does not have an R^2 statistic. This causes a lot of confusion; that is why I showed the appropriately named 'confusion matrix'. Remember (from OLS) R^2 is the shared variance between the actual dependent variable and the predicted dependent variable. The more variance these two share the closer the predicted and actual dependent variables are. Remember OLS outputs an estimated dependent variable. Logistic regression does NOT output an estimated dependent variable. The actual dependent variable is 0 or 1. The 'logit' is the natural log of the event /(1 – event). So there can be no 'estimated' dependent variable. If you HAVE to have some measure of goodness of fit I'd suggest using the log likelihood on the covariate and intercept. SPSS and SAS both output the –2LL on the intercept only and the –2LL on the intercept and covariates. Think of the –2LL on intercept as TSS (total sum of squares) and –2LL on intercept and covariates as RSS (regression sum of squares). R^2 is RSS / TSS and this will give an indication (called a pseudo-R^2) for those that need that metric.

Scoring the database with probability formula

Typically after a logistic regression is run, especially in a database marketing process, the model has to be applied to score the database. Yes, SAS now has 'proc score' but I want you to be able to do it yourself and to understand what's happening. It's old fashioned but you will know more.

Say we have the below (Table 5.7) model with probability to purchase. That is, the dependent variable is purchase = 1 for the event and purchase = 0 for the non-event. Because of the logistic curve bounding between 0 and 1, the formula is probability = $1/(1 + e^{-Z})$ where $Z = \alpha + \beta X_i$. For the above model this means:

$$\text{Probability} = 1/(1 + 2.71828 \wedge - (4.566 + X1 * -0.003 + x2 * 1.265 + x3 * 0.003))$$

This returns a probability between 0% and 100% for each customer (2.71828 = e). So apply this formula to your database and each customer will have a score (that can be used for a lift chart, see above) for probability to purchase.

Table 5.7   Probability to purchase

Independent variable	Parameter estimate
Intercept	4.566
X1	–0.003
X2	1.265
X3	0.003

USING LOGISTIC REGRESSION FOR MARKET BASKET ANALYSIS

Abstract

In general, market basket analysis is a backward-looking exercise. It uses descriptive analysis (frequencies, correlation, mathematical KPIs, etc) and outputs those products that tend to be purchased together. That gives no insights into what marketers should do with that output. Predictive analytics, using logistic regression, shows how much the probability of a product purchase increases/decreases given another product purchase. This gives marketers a strategic lever to use in bundling, etc.

What is a market basket?

In economics, a market basket is a fixed collection of items that consumers buy. This is used for metrics like CPI (inflation), etc. In marketing, a market basket is any two or more items bought together.

Market basket analysis is used, especially in retail/CPG, to bundle and offer promotions and gain insight in shopping/purchasing patterns. 'Market basket analysis' does not, by itself, describe HOW the analysis is done. That is, there is no associated technique with those words.

How is it usually done?

There are three general uses of data: descriptive, predictive and prescriptive. Descriptive is about the past, predictive uses statistical analysis to calculate a change on an output variable (eg, sales) given a change in an input variable (say, price) and prescriptive is a system that tries to optimize some metric (typically profit, etc). Descriptive data (means, frequencies, KPIs, etc) is a necessary, but not usually sufficient, step. Always get to at least the predictive step as soon as possible. Note that predictive here does not necessarily mean forecasted into the future. Structural analysis uses models to simulate the market, and estimate (predict) what causes what to happen. That is, using regression, a change in price shows what is the estimated (predicted) change in sales.

Market basket analysis often uses descriptive techniques. Sometimes it is just a 'report' of what per cent of items are purchased together. Affinity analysis (a slight step above) is mathematical, not statistical. Affinity analysis simply calculates the per cent of time combinations of products are purchased together. Obviously there is no probability involved. It is concerned with the rate of products purchased together, and not with a distribution around that association. It is very common and very useful but NOT predictive – therefore NOT so actionable.

Logistic regression

Let's talk about logistic regression. This is an ancient and well-known statistical technique, probably the analytic pillar upon which database marketing has been built. It is similar to ordinary regression in that there is a dependent variable that depends on one or more independent variables. There is a coefficient (although interpretation is not the same) and there is a (type of) t-test around each independent variable for significance.

The differences are that the dependent variable is binary (having two values, 0 or 1) in logistic and continuous in ordinary regression and to interpret the coefficients requires exponentiation. Because the dependent variable is binary, the result is heteroskedasticity. There is no (real) R^2, and 'fit' is about classification.

How to estimate/predict the market basket

The use of logistic regression in terms of market basket becomes obvious when it is understood that the predicted dependent variable is a probability. The formula to estimate probability from logistic regression is:

$$P_{(i)} = 1 / 1 + e^{-Z}$$

where $Z = \alpha + \beta X_i$. This means that the independent variables can be products purchased in a market basket to predict likelihood to purchase another product as the dependent variable. The above means to specifically take each (major) category of product (focus driven by strategy) and running a separate model for each, putting in all significant other products as independent variables. For example, say we have only three products, x, y and z. The idea is to design three models and test significance of each, meaning using logistic regression:

$$x = f(y,z)$$
$$y = f(x,z)$$
$$z = f(x,y).$$

Of course other variables can go into the model as appropriate but the interest is whether or not the independent (product) variables are significant in predicting (and to what extent) the probability of purchasing the dependent product variable. Of course, after significance is achieved, the insights generated are around the sign of the independent variable, ie, does the independent product increase or decrease the probability of purchasing the dependent product.

An example

As a simple example, say we are analysing a retail store, with categories of products like consumer electronics, women's accessories, newborn and infant items, etc. Thus, using logistic regression, a series of models should be run. That is:

consumer electronics = f(women's accessories, jewellery
and watches, furniture, entertainment, etc)

This means the independent variables are binary, coded as a '1' if the customer bought that category and a '0' if not. Table 5.8 details the output for all of the models. Note that other independent variables can be included in the model, if significant. These would often be seasonality, consumer confidence, promotions sent, etc.

To interpret, look at, say, the home décor model. If a customer bought consumer electronics, that increases the probability of buying home décor by 29%. If a customer bought newborn/infant items, that decreases the probability of buying home décor by 37%. If a customer bought furniture, that increases the probability of buying home décor by 121%. This has implications, especially for bundling and messaging. That is, offering, say, home décor and furniture together makes great sense, but offering home décor and newborn/infant items does not make sense.

Table 5.8 Associated probabilities

	Consumer electronics	Women's accessories	Newborn, infant, etc	Jewellery, watches	Furniture	Home décor	Entertainment	Sporting goods
Consumer electronics	XXX	Insig	Insig	−23%	34%	26%	98%	12%
Women's accessories	Insig	XXX	39%	68%	22%	21%	Insig	−31%
Newborn, infant, etc	Insig	43%	XXX	−11%	−21%	−31%	29%	−34%
Jewellery, watches	−29%	71%	−22%	XXX	12%	24%	−11%	−34%
Furniture	31%	18%	−17%	9%	XXX	115%	37%	29%
Home décor	29%	24%	−37%	21%	121%	XXX	31%	12%
Entertainment	85%	Insig	31%	−9%	41%	29%	XXX	31%
Sporting goods	18%	−37%	−29%	−29%	24%	9%	33%	XXX

And here is a special note about products purchased together. If it is known, via the above, that home décor and furniture tend to go together, these can be and should be bundled together, messaged together, etc. But there is no reason to PROMOTE them together or to discount them together because they are purchased together anyway.

Conclusion

The above detailed a simple (and more powerful way) to do market basket analysis. If given a choice, always go beyond mere descriptive techniques and apply predictive techniques.

Checklist

You'll be the smartest person in the room if you:

☐ Can differentiate between logistic and ordinary regression. Logistic and ordinary regression are similar in that both are single equations having a dependent variable explained by one or more independent variables. They are dissimilar in that ordinary regression has a continuous dependent variable while logistic regression has a binary variable; ordinary regression uses least squares to estimate the coefficients while logistic regression uses maximum likelihood.

☐ Remember that logistic regression predicts a probability of an event.

☐ Always test for outliers/influential observations using z-scores.

☐ Point out that the 'confusion matrix' is a means of goodness of fit.

☐ Observe that lift/gains charts are used as a measure of modelling efficacy as well as (eg, in direct mail) depth of mailing.

☐ Remember to always check/correct for collinearity.

☐ Suggest logistic regression as a way to model market baskets.

When are my customers most likely to buy?

06

Introduction

Survival analysis is an especially interesting and powerful technique. In terms of marketing science it is relatively new, mostly getting exposure in these last 20 years or so. It answers a very important and particular question: 'WHEN is an event (purchase, response, churn, etc) most likely to occur?' I'd submit this is a more relevant question than 'HOW LIKELY is an event (purchase, response, churn, etc) to occur?' That is, a customer may be VERY likely to purchase but not for 10 months. Is timing information of value? Of course it is; remember, time is money.

Beware though. Given the increase in actionable information, it should be no surprise that survival analysis is more complex than logistic regression. Remember how much more complex logistic regression was than ordinary regression?

Conceptual overview of survival analysis

Survival analysis (via proportional hazards modelling) was essentially invented by Sir David Cox in 1972 with his seminal and oft-quoted paper, 'Regression models and life tables' in the *Journal of the Royal Statistical Society* (Cox, 1972). It's important to note this technique was specifically designed to study time until event problems. This came out of biostatistics and the event of study was typically death. That's why it's called 'survival analysis'. Get it?

The general use case was in drug treatment. There would be, say, a drug study where a panel was divided into two groups; one group got the new drug and the other group did not. Every month the test subjects were called and asked for updates, tracking their survival. There would be two curves developed, one following the treatment group and another following the non-treatment group. If the treatment tended to work the time until event (death) was increased.

One major issue involved censored observations. It's an easy matter to compare the average survival times of the treatment vs the non-treatment group.

Censored observation: that observation wherein we do not know its status. Typically the event has not occurred yet or was lost in some way.

But what about those subjects that dropped out of the study because they moved away or lost contact? Or the study ended and not everyone has died yet? Each of these involves censored observations. The question about what to do with these kinds of observations is why Cox regression was created; a non-parametric partial likelihood technique, which he called proportional hazards. It deals with censored observations, which are those patients that have an unknown time until event status. This unknown time until event can be caused by either not having the event at the time of the analysis or losing contact with the patient.

What about those subjects that died from another cause and not the cause the test drug was treating? Are there other variables (covariates) that influence (increase or decrease) the time until the event? These questions involve extensions of the general survival model. The first is about competing risks and the second is about regression involving independent variables. These will be dealt with soon enough.

BUSINESS CASE

At the end of the year Scott called his team and the marketing organization together for a review and brainstorming exercise. This is something Scott believed every smart analytics pro should do. He was especially interested in how the analytics team was perceived as providing value last year and what might be done differently in the upcoming year.

During the meeting the marketing managers complimented Scott and his team for providing actionable insights. The results gave most of them a good bonus and they wanted to get another one this year. They did not all completely understand the technical details and Scott made the culture around that okay. He tried to make his team viewed as consultants; accessible, conversational and engaged with the broader organization.

'Thanks', Scott said and turned to the director of consumer marketing, Stacy. 'Where can we improve? What targeting would help you and your team?'

'Well, we have a pretty good process now. We pull lists based on likelihood to respond. It's worked well.'

'Yeah, I'm glad of that. The lift charts from logit helped us mail only as deep as we needed to.'

'This gives us the best ROI in the company.'

'But is that all we can do? Just target those most likely to respond?' Scott asked.

'What else is there?' Stacy asked, checking her phone.

'Yeah, I'm not sure', Scott said. 'What do you need to know to do your job? What if there were no restrictions on data or feasibility or anything else? You have a magic button that if you push it you would know the one thing that would allow you to do your job better, better than ever before, a knowledge that gives you a tremendous advantage.'

'Easy!' Kristina said. 'If I knew what product each customer would purchase in what order, that is, if I knew WHEN he would purchase a desktop, or a notebook, I would not send a lot of useless catalogues or e-mails to him. I'd send him the most compelling marcom at just the right time with just the right promotion and just the right messaging to maximize his purchase.'

They all looked at her. Then they nodded their heads. Kristina had talked with Scott about joining his team after she graduates.

'It sounds like science fiction', Stacy said. 'We would get a list of customers with a most likely time to purchase each product?'

Scott rubbed his chin. 'Yes. It's a prediction of when each customer is going to purchase each product.'

'But', said Mark, 'what does that mean? Before?' Mark was an analyst on Scott's team. 'We want to predict when they'll purchase?'

'I think so', Scott said. 'Predict when they'll buy a desktop, when they'll buy a notebook, etc.'

'Imagine having the database scored with the number of days until each customer is likely to buy personal electronics, a desktop, etc.' Kristina said. 'We'd just sort the database by products and those more likely to buy sooner would get the communication.'

'But does that mean using regression, or logit, or what?'

'I don't know', Scott said. 'What do we do about predicting those who have not purchased a product? Is this probability to buy at each distinct time period?'

They all left the meeting excited about the new metric (time until purchase) but Scott was wondering what technique would answer that question. If they used ordinary regression, the dependent variable would be 'number of days until purchase of a desktop' based on some zero-day, say January first two years ago. Those that purchased a desktop would have the event at that many days. Those that did not purchase a desktop gave Scott a choice. Either he would cap the number of days at now, say two years from the zero date, which means, say, 725, if they were on file from the zero date onward. That is, those that have not purchased a desktop would be forced to have the event at 725 days. Not a good choice. The other option would be to delete those that did not purchase a desktop. Also not a good choice.

Rule *numero uno*: never ever under any circumstances delete data. Never. Ever. This is an 'Off with their heads!' crime (unless of course the data is wrong or an outlier).

Ignoring the time until the event-dependent variable could give rise to logistic regression. That is, those receiving a 1 if they did purchase a desktop and a 0 if they did not. This puts him right back into probability, and they all agreed that timing was a more strategic option. So Scott concluded that both OLS and logit have severe faults in terms of time until event problems.

It's important to make a clarification about a trap a lot of people fall into. Survival analysis is a technique specifically designed to estimate and understand time until event problems. The underlying assumption is that each time period is independent of each other time period. That is, the prediction has no 'memory'. Some under-educated/under-experienced analysts think that if we are, say, trying to predict what month an event will happen they can do 12 logits and have one model for January, another for February, etc. The collected data would have a 1 if the customer purchased in January and a 0 if not, likewise, if the model was for

February a customer would have a 1 if they purchased in February and a 0 if not. This seems like it would work, right? Wrong. February is not independent of January. In order for the customer to buy in February they had to decide NOT to buy in January. See? This is why logit is inappropriate.

Now for you academicians, yes, logistic regression is appropriate for a small subset of a particular problem. If the data is periodic (an event that can only occur at regular and specific intervals) then, yes, logistic regression can be used to estimate survival analyses. This requires a whole different kind of dataset, one where each row is not a customer but a time period with an event. I'd still suggest even then, why not just use survival analysis (in SAS lifereg or phreg)?

More about survival analysis

As mentioned, survival analysis came from biostatistics in the early 1970s, where the subject studied was an event: death. Survival analysis is about modelling the time until an event. In biostatistics the event is typically death but in marketing the event can be response, purchase, churn, etc.

Due to the nature of survival studies, there are a couple of characteristics that are endemic to this technique. As alluded to earlier, the dependent variable is time until event, so time is built into the analysis. The second endemic thing to survival analysis is observations that are censored. A censored observation is either an observation that has not had the event or an observation that was lost to the study and there is no knowledge of having the event or not – but we do know at some point in time that the observation has not had the event.

In marketing it's common for the event to be a purchase. Imagine scoring a database of customers with time until purchase. That is far more actionable than, from logistic regression, probability of purchase.

Let's talk about censored observations. What can be done about them? Remember we do not know what happened to these observations. We could delete them. That would be simple, but depending how many there are that might be throwing away a lot of data. Also, they might be the most interesting data of all, so deleting them is probably a bad idea. (And, remember the 'Off with their heads!' crime mentioned previously.) We could just give the maximum time until an event to all those that have not had the event. This would also be a bad idea, especially if a large portion of the sample is censored, as is often the case. (It can be shown that throwing away a lot of censored data will bias any results.) Thus, we need a technique that can deal with censored data. Also, deleting censored observations ignores a lot of information. While we don't know when (or even if) the customer, say, purchased, we do know as of a certain time that they did NOT purchase. So we have part of their curve, part of their information, part of their behaviour. This should not ever be deleted. This is why Cox invented partial likelihood.

Figure 6.1   General survival curve

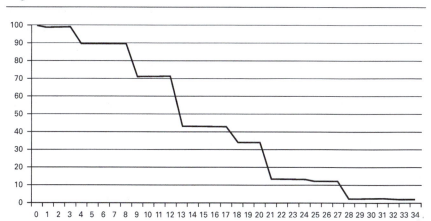

Figure 6.1 is a general survival curve. The vertical axis is a count of those in the 'risk set' and it starts out with 100%. That is, at time 0 everyone is 'at risk' of having the event and no one has had the event. At day 1, that is, after one day, one person died (had the event) and there are now 99 that are at risk. No one died for 3 days until 9 had the event at day 5, etc. Note that at about day 12, 29 had the event.

Now note Figure 6.2. One survival curve is the same as above, but the other one is 'further out'. Note that 50% of the first curve is reached at 14 days, but the second curve does not reach 50% until 28 days. That is, they 'live longer'.

Figure 6.2   Survival analysis

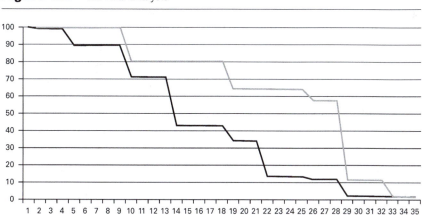

Survival analysis is a type of regression, but with a twist. It does not use maximum likelihood, but partial likelihood. (The most common form of survival analysis, proportional hazards, uses partial likelihood.) The dependent variable is now two parts: time until the event and whether the event has occurred or not. This allows the use of censored observations.

The above graphs are survival graphs. Much of Cox regression is not about the survival curve, but the hazard rate. The hazard is nearly the reciprocal of the survival curve. This ends up as the instantaneous risk that an event will occur at some particular time. Think of metrics like miles per hour as analogous to the hazard rate. At 40 miles per hour you will travel 40 miles in one hour if speed remains the same. The hazard quantifies the rate of the event in each period of time.

SAS does both survival modelling (with proc lifereg) and hazard modelling (as proc phreg). SPSS only does hazard modelling (as Cox regression). Lifereg does left and interval censoring while phreg does only right censoring (this is not usually an issue for marketing). With lifereg a distribution must be specified, but with phreg (as it's semi-parametric) there is no distribution. This is one of the advantages of phreg. The other advantage of phreg is that it incorporates time-varying independent variables, while lifereg does not. (This also is not usually much of an issue for marketing.)

I typically use lifereg as it easily outputs a time until event prediction, it is on the survival curve and it is relatively easy to understand and interpret. That's what we'll demonstrate here.

I might mention that survival analysis is not just about the time until event prediction. As with all regressions the independent variables are strategic levers. Say we find that for every 1,000 e-mails we send purchases tend to happen three days sooner. Do you see the financial implications here? How valuable is it to know you have incentivized a group of customers in making purchases earlier? If this does not interest you then you are in the wrong career field.

Model output and interpretation

So Scott's team investigated survival analysis and concluded it was worth a shot. It seemed to give a way to answer the key question, 'WHEN is a customer most likely to purchase a desktop?'

Table 6.1 lists the final desktop model using lifereg. The variables are all significant at the 95% level. The first column is the name of the independent variable. The interpretation of lifereg coefficients requires transformations. This gets the parameter estimates into a form to make strategic interpretation.

The next column is the beta coefficient. This is what SAS outputs but, as with logistic regression, is not very meaningful. A negative coefficient tends to bring the event of a desktop purchase in; a positive coefficient tends to push the event (desktop purchase) out. This is a regression output so in that regard interpretation is the same, *ceteris paribus*.

To get per cent impacts on time to/until event (TTE), each beta coefficient must be exponentiated, e^B. That's the third column. The next column subtracts 1 from it and converts it into a percentage. Note that, for example, 'recent online visit'

Table 6.1 Final desktop model, lifereg

Independent variable	Beta	e^B	(e^B)-1	Avg TTE
Any previous purchase	−0.001	0.999	−0.001	−0.012
Recent online visit	−0.014	0.987	−0.013	−0.148
# Direct mails	0.157	1.17	0.17	1.865
# E-mails opened	−0.011	0.989	−0.011	−0.12
# E-mails clicked	−0.033	0.968	−0.032	−0.352
Income	−0.051	0.95	−0.05	−0.547
Size household	−0.038	0.963	−0.037	−0.408
Education	−0.023	0.977	−0.023	−0.249
Blue collar occupation	0.151	1.163	0.163	1.792
# Promotions sent	−0.006	0.994	−0.006	−0.066
Purch desktop < year	2.09	8.085	7.085	77.934

e^Beta is a 0.987 impact on time, or, if 1 is subtracted shows a 1.3% decrease in average TTE. To convert that to a scale – say the average is 11 weeks – this means −0.013 * 11 = −0.148 weeks. The interpretation is that if a customer had a recent online visit, that tends to pull in (shorten) TTE by 0.148 weeks. Not really impactful but it makes sense, right?

Notice the last variable, 'purch desktop < year'. See how it's positive, 2.09? This means if the customer has purchased a desktop in the last year the time until (another) desktop purchase is pushed out by ((e^B)−1)*11 = 77.934 weeks. See how this works? See how strategically insightful survival analysis can be? You can build a business case around marcom sent (cost of marcom) and decreasing the time until purchase (revenue realized sooner).

As typically used on a database, each customer is scored with time until the event, in this case, time until a desktop purchase. The database is sorted and a list is designed with those most likely to purchase next (see Table 6.2). This time to event (TTE) is at the (50% decile) median.

Note that customer 1000 is expected to purchase a desktop in 3.3 weeks and customer 1030 is expected to purchase a desktop in 14.9 weeks. Using survival analysis (in SAS, proc lifereg) allowed Scott's team to score the database with those likely to purchase sooner. This list is more actionable than using logistic regression, where the score is just probability to purchase.

Now let's talk about competing risks. While survival analysis is about death, the study usually is interested in ONE kind of death, or death from ONE cause. That is,

Table 6.2   Time to event (in weeks)

Customer ID	TTE
1000	3.365
1002	3.702
1004	4.072
1006	4.479
1011	5.151
1013	5.923
1015	6.812
1017	7.834
1022	9.009
1024	10.36
1026	12.43
1030	14.92

the biostat study is about, say, death by heart attack and not about death by cancer or death by a car accident. But it's true that in a study of death by heart attack a patient is also at risk for other kinds of death. This is called competing risks.

In the marketing arena, while the focus might be on a purchase event for, say, a desktop PC, the customer is also 'at risk' for purchasing other things, like a notebook or consumer electronics. Fortunately, this is an easy job of just coding the events of interest. That is, Scott can code for an event as DT (desktop) purchase, with all else coded as a non-event. He can do another model as a purchase event of, say, notebooks, and all else is a non-event, that is, all other things are censored. Thus Table 6.3 shows three models, having a purchase event for desktop, notebook and consumer electronics.

A little technical background

First, something to note about lifereg is that it requires you to give it a distribution. (Phreg does not require that you give it a distribution, something a lot of analysts like.) In using lifereg, I'd suggest testing all distributions, and the one that fits the best (lowest BIC or log likelihood) is the one to use. Another view would be to acknowledge that the distribution has a shape and ascertain what shape makes sense given the data you're using.

Table 6.3 Three model comparison

Customer ID	TT desktop purch	TT notebook purch	TT consumer electronics purch
1000	3.365	75.66	39.51
1002	3.702	88.2	45.95
1004	4.072	111.2	55.66
1006	4.479	15.05	19.66
1011	5.151	13.07	9.109
1013	5.923	9.945	7.934
1015	6.812	22.24	144.5
1017	7.834	3.011	5.422
1022	9.009	2.613	5.811
1024	10.36	1.989	6.174
1026	12.43	4.448	8.44
1030	14.92	0.602	7.76

Pseudo R^2

While R^2 as a metric makes no sense (same as with logistic regression) a lot of analysts like some kind of R^2. To review, R^2 in OLS is the shared variance between the actual dependent variable and the predicted dependent variable. In survival analysis there is no predicted dependent variable. Most folks use the median as the prediction and that's okay. I'd suggest running a simple model with, and without, covariates. That is, in SAS with proc lifereg, run the model without the covariates (independent variables) and collect the –2LL stat. Then run the model with the covariates and collect the –2LL stat and divide. This metric (by analogy) shows the per cent of explained over the per cent unexplained.

Conclusion

Survival analysis is not a common topic in marketing analytics and it should be. While it's true that marketers and biostatisticians (where survival analysis originated) do not move in the same circles, I've now given you some of the basics, so go and get to work.

LIFETIME VALUE: HOW PREDICTIVE ANALYSIS IS SUPERIOR TO DESCRIPTIVE ANALYSIS

Abstract

Typically lifetime value (LTV) is but a calculation using historical data. This calculation makes some rather heroic assumptions to project into the future but gives no insights into why a customer is lower valued, or how to make a customer higher valued. Using predictive techniques, here survival analysis gives an indication as to what causes purchases to happen sooner, and thus how to increase LTV.

Descriptive analysis

Lifetime value (LTV) is typically done as just a calculation, using past (historical) data. That is, it's only descriptive.

While there are many versions of LTV (depending on data, industry, interest, etc) the following is conceptually applied to all. LTV, via descriptive analysis, works as follows:

1 It uses historical data to sum up each customer's total revenue.
2 This sum then has subtracted from it some costs: typically cost to serve, cost to market, cost of goods sold, etc.
3 This net revenue is then converted into an annual average amount and depicted as a cash flow.
4 These cash flows are assumed to continue into the future and diminish over time (depending on durability, sales cycle, etc). Often decreasing arbitrarily by say 10% each year until they are effectively zero.
5 These (future, diminished) cash flows are then summed up and discounted (usually by weighted average cost of capital) to get their net present value (NPV).
6 This NPV is called LTV. This calculation is applied to each customer.

Thus each customer has a value associated with it. The typical use is for marketers to find the 'high-valued' customers (based on past purchases). These high-valued customers get most of the communications, promotions/ discounts and marketing efforts. Descriptive analysis is merely about targeting those already engaged, much like RFM (recency, frequency, monetary), which we will discuss later.

This seems to be a good starting point but, as is usual with descriptive analysis, contributes nothing informative. Why is one customer more valuable, and will they continue to be? Is it possible to extract additional value, but at what cost? Is it possible to garner more revenue from a lower-valued customer because they are more loyal or cost less to serve? What part of the marketing mix is each customer most sensitive to? LTV (as described above) gives no implications for strategy. The only strategy is to offer and promote to (only) the high-valued customers.

Predictive analysis

How would LTV change using predictive analysis instead of descriptive analysis? First note that while LTV is a future-oriented metric, descriptive analysis uses historical (past) data and the entire metric is built on that, with assumptions about the future applied unilaterally to every customer. Predictive analysis specifically thrusts LTV into the future (where it belongs) by using independent variables to predict the next time until purchase. Since the major customer behaviour driving LTV is timing, amount and number of purchases, a statistical technique needs to be used that predicts time until an event. (Ordinary regression predicting the LTV amount ignores timing and number of purchases.)

Survival analysis is a technique designed specifically to study time until event problems. It has timing built into it and thus a future view is already embedded in the algorithm. This removes much of the arbitrariness of typical (descriptive) LTV calculations.

So, what about using survival analysis to see which independent variables, say, bring in a purchase? Decreasing time until purchase tends to increase LTV. While survival analysis can predict the next time until purchase, the strategic value of survival analysis is in using the independent variables to CHANGE the timing of purchases. That is, descriptive analysis shows what happened; predictive analysis gives a glimpse of what might CHANGE the future.

Strategy using LTV dictates understanding the causes of customer value: why a customer purchases, what increases/decreases the time until purchase, probability of purchasing at future times, etc. Then when these insights are learned, marketing levers (shown as independent variables) are exploited to extract additional value from each customer. This means knowing that one customer is, say, sensitive to price and that a discount will tend to decrease their time until purchase. That is, they will purchase sooner (maybe purchase larger total amounts and maybe purchase more often) with a discount. Another customer prefers, say, product X and product Y bundled together to increase the probability of purchase and this bundling decreases their time until purchase. This insight allows different strategies for different customer needs and sensitivities. Survival analysis applied to each customer yields insights to understand and incentivize changes in behaviour.

This means just assuming the past behaviour will continue into the future (as descriptive analysis does) with no idea why, is no longer necessary. It's possible for descriptive and predictive analysis to give contradictory answers. Which is why 'crawling' might be detrimental to 'walking'.

If a firm can get a customer to purchase sooner, there is an increased chance of adding purchases – depending on the product. But even if the number of purchases is not increased, the firm getting revenue sooner will add to their financial value (time is money).

Also a business case can be created by showing the trade-off in giving up, say, margin but obtaining revenue faster. This means strategy can revolve around maximization of cost balanced against customer value.

The idea is to model next time until purchase, the baseline, and see how to improve that. How is this carried out? A behaviourally-based method would be to segment the customers (based on behaviour), apply a survival model to each segment and score each individual customer. By behaviour we typically mean purchasing (amount, timing, share of products, etc) metrics and marcom (open and click, direct mail coupons, etc) responses.

An example

Let's use an example. Table 6.4 shows two customers from two different behavioural segments. Customer XXX purchases every 88 days with an annual revenue of 43,958, costs of 7,296 for a net revenue of 36,662. Say the second year is exactly the same. So year one discounted at 9% is NPV of 33,635 and year two discounted at 9% for two years is 30,857 for a total LTV of 64,492. Customer YYY has similar calculations for LTV of 87,898.

The above (using descriptive analysis) would have marketers targeting customer YYY with > 23,000 value over customer XXX. But do we know

Table 6.4 Comparison of customers from different behavioural segments

Customer	Days between purchases	Annual purchases	Total revenue	Total costs	Net rev YR 1	Net rev YR 2	YR1 Disc	YR2 Disc	LTV at 9%
XXX	88	4.148	43,958	7,296	36,662	36,662	33,635	30,857	64,492
YYY	58	6.293	62,289	12,322	49,967	49,967	45,842	42,056	87,898

anything about WHY customer XXX is so much lower valued? Is there anything that can be done to make them higher valued?

Applying a survival model to each segment outputs independent variables and shows their effect on the dependent variable. In this case the dependent variable is (average) time until purchase. Say the independent variables (which defined the behavioural segments) are things like price discounts, product bundling, seasonal messages, adding additional direct mail catalogues and offering online exclusives. The segmentation should separate customers based on behaviour and the survival models should show how different levels of independent variables drive different strategies.

Table 6.5 below shows results of survival modelling on the two different customers that come from two different segments. The independent variables are price discounts of 10%, product bundling, etc. The TTE is time to event and shows what happens to time until purchase based on changing one of the independent variables. For example, for customer XXX, giving a price discount of 10% on average decreases their time until purchase by 14 days. Giving YYY a 10% discount decreases their time until purchase by

Table 6.5 Results of survival modelling

	XXX	**YYY**
Variables	TTE	TTE
Price discount 10%	−14	−2
Product bundling	−4	12
Seasonal message	6	5
Five more catalogues	11	−2
Online exclusive	−11	3

only 2 days. This means XXX is far more sensitive to price then YYY – which would not be known by descriptive analysis alone. Likewise giving XXX more direct mail catalogues pushes out their TTE but pulls in YYY by 2 days. Note also that very little of the marketing levers affect YYY very much. We are already getting nearly all from YYY that we can, and no marketing effort does very much to impact the TTE. However, with XXX there are several things that can be done to bring in their purchases. Again, none of these would be known without survival modelling on each behavioural segment.

Table 6.6 below shows new LTV calculations on XXX after using survival modelling results. We decreased TTE by 24 days, by using some combinations of discounts, bundling and online exclusives, etc. Note now the LTV for XXX (after using predictive analysis) is greater than YYY.

What survival analysis offers, in addition to marketing strategy levers, is a financial optimal scenario, particularly in terms of costs to market. That is, customer XXX responds to a discount. It's possible to calculate and test what is the (just) needed threshold of discounts to bring a purchase in by so many days with the estimated level of revenue. This ends up being a cost/benefit analysis that makes marketers think about strategy. This is the advantage of predictive analysis – giving marketers strategic options.

Table 6.6   LTV calculations

Customer	Days between purchases	Annual purchases	Total revenue	Total costs	Net rev YR 1	Net rev YR 2	YR1 Disc	YR2 Disc	LTV at 9%
XXX	64	5.703	60,442	10,032	50,410	50,410	33,635	30,857	88,677
YYY	58	6.293	62,289	12,322	49,967	49,967	45,842	42,056	87,898

Checklist

You'll be the smartest person in the room if you:

☐ Point out that 'time until an event' is a more relevant marketing question than 'probability of an event'.

☐ Remember that survival analysis came out of biostatistics and is somewhat rare in marketing, but very powerful.

☐ Observe that there are two 'flavours' of survival analysis: lifereg and proportional hazards. Lifereg models the survival curve and proportional hazards models the hazard rate.

☐ Champion competing risks, a natural output of survival analysis. In marketing, this gives time until various events or time until multiple products purchased, etc.

☐ Understand that predictive lifetime value (using survival analysis) is more insightful than descriptive lifetime value.

Panel regression 07

How to use a cross-sectional time series

Introduction

Most dependent variable frameworks either have each row as a cross section or each row as a time period – but not both. Cross sections are usually ordinary regression and time periods are usually auto regression. If a framework included both, better estimates and better insights should result. These improved estimates come from the additional informational content supplied in the variance from both cross sections and time periods.

So what is meant by cross section? Cross section is analysis by customer, by store, by geography, etc. Then time series data on each cross section, whether it is sales, media, promotions or some other stimuli, could be used as independent variables. The power of panel regression is in using both cross section and time series observations accounting for both cross-sectional and time series impacts (see Table 7.1).

The following shows a common problem in analytics: accounting for geographical variance (which could also be same county sales or same customer, etc), solved by taking into account both differences in counties and differences in time series on sales, promotions, media, etc.

Panel regression specifically analyses cross-sectional time series data. It incorporates these effects into the model. It also increases the sample size, which may or may not be a trivial benefit. And panel models (especially fixed effects) can control for unobserved heterogeneity, which may be critical.

The business problem addressed here is county (geographic region) influence. This is an important business driver for companies and the source and focus of a large amount of analysis.

Typical examples of geo-analyses include demand (by, say, county) and marcom (marketing communication)/media (by time period). There is a need to incorporate information from both a cross section and a time series point of view.

County modelling is about measuring change in a county over time. To incorporate both by-county and over-time impacts, something other than ordinary regression (time series or not) needs to be incorporated. That is, if the approach is by county (each row is a county) then the impact of over time is lost. If the approach is time series (each row is a time period) then the county data are aggregated and the by-county impact is lost.

Another common issue with regression frameworks is a hidden/unobserved variable that impacts sales. That is, there may be another variable (competitive moves, socio-demographics, etc) that the firm cannot account for (does not have an explanatory variable). Ordinary least squares (OLS) will be biased if used. Panel regression can account for it and partial out its effects.

Thus, the goal is to measure the impact of different types of media by county over time. This can result in a plan to optimally spend (media, marcom, etc) where it has the most impact.

What is panel regression?

Most data are either cross-sectional or longitudinal. Panel data refers to multi-dimensional data that is BOTH cross-sectional and time series. Thus, panel analysis is cross-sectional longitudinal data.

There are three general types of longitudinal data:

1 Time series data: many observations on as few as one cross section, eg, stock market prices, summary units sold by week, etc.

2 Pooled cross sections: two or more samples of many cross sections, eg, social/population surveys, geographic or segment revenue, etc.

3 Panel data: two or more observations on two or more cross sections, eg, time series data on firms or organizations at different points in time, aggregate regional or segment data over time, etc.

Panel modelling is about describing changes (on a cross section) over time. For example, how do different levels and types of media drive county sales given seasonality? These causal models explain policy evaluation and estimation of treatment effects.

Cross sections (also called groups or even units) are the sample of observations: stores, customers, segments, zip codes, households, etc. That is, any group that can have multiple observations over time can work as panel data.

A key issue, more an econometric than a business one, is unobserved heterogeneity. That is, the possibility of another cause or a missing variable or something impacting the dependent variable that no data is available to express. Panel modelling allows the effects of the unobserved heterogeneity to be included. If the unobserved cross section-specific effects are treated as constants, then this is the fixed effects model. If the unobserved cross section-specific effects are treated as random, then this is the random effects model.

Panel regression: details

The data structure

To get a visual idea of panel data structure, see Table 7.1. Each county is a cross section and each quarter is a time period. Note that the cross section is repeated eight times, one for each quarter representing two years of data. The independent variables are number of direct mails (DM), number of e-mails (EM) and number of short message service (SMS, ie, text messages), sent to that county's customers for each time period. We want to know how these marketing communications affect each county's revenue (the dependent variable) over time.

The fixed effects model

This is a model with constant slopes but intercepts that differ according to cross section (group, unit, customer, store, county) and/or time periods. Thus, this model is essentially an OLS dummy variable model in that a dummy variable is applied to every cross section and/or every time period:

$$Y_{it} = a_i + X^t_{it}B + e_{it}$$

Table 7.1   Panel data structure

COUNTY	QRTR	REVENUE	# DM	# EM	# SMS
1000	1	$12,450	48	214	13
1000	2	$135,750	147	226	38
1000	3	$155,887	183	228	46
1000	4	$225,125	357	237	101
1000	5	$13,073	60	214	13
1000	6	$142,538	147	227	41
1000	7	$163,681	184	230	54
1000	8	$236,381	445	239	114
1001	1	$11,205	48	213	12
1001	2	$122,175	118	224	32
1001	3	$140,298	146	226	40
1001	4	$202,613	356	236	90
1001	5	$11,765	48	214	13
1001	6	$128,284	147	225	36
1001	7	$147,313	147	227	42
1001	8	$212,743	358	236	93
1002	1	$14,006	60	215	14
1002	2	$152,719	147	227	43
1002	3	$175,373	229	231	61
1002	4	$253,266	503	240	123
1002	5	$14,707	60	215	14
1002	6	$160,355	183	229	50
1002	7	$184,142	229	232	67
1002	8	$265,929	524	241	133
1003	1	$25,000	75	218	20
1003	2	$35,000	93	219	22
1003	3	$75,000	94	220	23
1003	4	$125,000	117	224	33
1003	5	$95,000	117	222	27
1003	6	$125,000	118	224	33
1003	7	$185,000	229	233	69
1003	8	$275,350	545	242	144
1004	1	$14,006	60	215	14

Y_{it} is the dependent variable, by subject i by time t, where a_i is the subject-specific intercept terms, X is the independent variable data by time and by subject and B is the coefficients on the independent variables.

Fixed effects models have some baggage. Due to the often large number of dummy variables, degrees of freedom plummet. This means the power of statistical tests is weak. Too many dummy variables also mean collinearity, which can change signs, increase standard errors and decrease power of statistical tests.

Yet the fixed effects model is a way to account for unobserved heterogeneity – which can be crucial.

The random effects model

This is a model that assumes the intercept is a random variable. The random outcome is a function of some mean value and a random error. This results in a cross-sectional error term, say V_i. This indicates the specific deviation from the constant of the cross section, which means the random error V_i is heterogeneity specific to the individual cross section. Note that this random error is constant over time. Therefore, the random error e_{it} is specific to a particular observation. The random effects model has the distinct advantage of allowing for time-invariant variables to be included among the independent variables:

$$Y_{it} = X^t_{it}B + a + u_i + e_{it}$$

Y_{it} is the dependent variable, by subject i by time t, where $a + u_i$ is the unobserved effect partitioned into a component that is common to all subjects and a disturbance that is subject specific, X is the independent variable data by time and by subject and B is the coefficients on the independent variables.

The coefficients are allowed to vary over the cross sections. This model allows both random intercept and independent variables to vary around common means. Thus, the random coefficients can be considered outcomes of a common mean and an error term, representing a mean deviation for each cross section.

Testing which effects to model

The Hausman specification test compares the fixed vs random effects under the null hypothesis that the individual effects are uncorrelated with the other regressors in the model. If correlated, Ho (null hypothesis) is rejected

(Pr > 0.05), meaning a random effects model produces biased estimators, so a fixed effects model is preferred.

The F-stat will test whether the fixed effects impacts are all zero. That is, Pr < 0.05 then the fixed effects model is inappropriate.

BUSINESS CASE

There has been a big push from strategy to incorporate geo-targeting into testing and predictions and even a possible retail rollout. The analytic question was to what extent did, say, counties explain sales volume. Scott knew the issue ended up being about the cost of marcom (marketing communications), especially direct mail. He proposed panel regression, which specifically accounts for the explanatory power of cross sections, in the case of counties and time series. He collected quarterly sales data.

The Hausman test indicated random effects were inappropriate so a fixed effects model was used. This means the coefficients on the marcom variables will be fixed and insights are gathered in terms of differing time series and differing cross-sectional groups.

Insights about marcom (direct mail, e-mail and SMS)

To show why the Hausman test is important, which shows which effects model is inappropriate, the coefficients on marcom using random effects are shown in Table 7.2.

Table 7.2 Coefficients on marcom: random effects

R^2	45.56%
PARAMETERS	EST
DM	2,335.6
EM	91.6
SMS	−6,848.8

Given that the Hausman test tells random effects is inappropriate, Table 7.3 shows the fixed effects for marcom.

The fit is much better using fixed effects and the insights from marcom make more sense. E-mail can be negative because of e-mail fatigue as shown in the fixed effects model. The random effects model had SMS as negative which is nonsensical and shows e-mail as positive.

Table 7.3 Coefficients on marcom: fixed effects

R^2	94.91%
PARAMETERS	EST
DM	1,960.6
EM	−297.4
SMS	5,679.4

Insights about time period (quarters)

Quarter 8 was removed (avoiding the dummy trap) and the resulting impacts of the quarters is insightful. Quarter 7 increases revenue on average by 19,000 and Quarter 5 decreases revenue on average by 50,000. All were significant.

Table 7.4 shows that the quarterly seasonality is important and predictable and has to be taken into account to confidently measure the marcom impact.

Table 7.4 Quarterly seasonality

PARAMETERS	EST
QRTR 1	−11,478
QRTR 2	6,705
QRTR 3	2,500
QRTR 4	1,247
QRTR 5	−50,000
QRTR 6	−9,056
QRTR 7	19,000

Insights about cross sections (counties)

All of the county variables were significant: some had a positive impact and some had a negative impact.

Table 7.5 shows the value of including cross-sectional analysis. This is an important insight. It means that the variance of revenue is accounted for, in part, by the variance of counties. There are significant differences in county performance that affect the impact that comes from marcom. To ignore county variance in the model would fit far worse and attribute too much impact to marcom. Meaning marcom would look more important than it really is.

Table 7.5 Cross-sectional analysis

PARAMETERS	EST
COUNTY 001	2,001
COUNTY 002	1,852
COUNTY 003	1,174
...	...
COUNTY 745	−116
COUNTY 746	−221
COUNTY 747	−409

Conclusion

Now Scott can show county sales as an effect of cross-sectional and time period variance. The assumption is that other factors, such as competitive density, trade area demographics, etc, are embedded in the county's impact on revenue. This can only be accurate if county variance and time variance is accounted for. Then the impact of different marcom vehicles, etc, can be assigned correctly. This can be best analysed via panel regression.

Checklist

You'll be the smartest person in the room if you:

☐ Understand when data can be longitudinal (cross-sectional and time series).

☐ Recognize the advantages of panel regression, incorporating BOTH cross-sectional and time series data.

☐ Remember there are three general forms of panel regression: fixed, random and mixed.

☐ Do test (using the Hausman and F-stat) to determine whether fixed or random effect is the better model.

☐ Realize that panel regression assumes most of the explanatory power comes from cross-sectional and time series data, NOT the independent variables.

Systems of equations for modelling dependent variable techniques

08

Introduction

So far we've dealt with one equation, a rather simple point of view. Of course, consumer behaviour is anything but simple. Marketing science is designed to understand, predict and ultimately incentivize/change consumer behaviour. This requires techniques that are as complicated as that behaviour is sophisticated. This is where simultaneous equations come in, as a more realistic model of behaviour.

> **Simultaneous equations:** a system of more than one dependent variable-type equation, often sharing several independent variables.

What are simultaneous equations?

Simply put, simultaneous equations are systems of equations. You had this in algebra. It's important. This begins to build a simulation of an entire process. It's done in macroeconomics (remember the Keynesian equations?) and it can be done in marketing.

Predetermined and exogenous variables

There are two kinds of variables: predetermined (lagged endogenous and exogenous) and endogenous variables. Generally, exogenous are variables determined OUTSIDE the system of equations and endogenous are determined INSIDE the system of equations. (Think of endogenous variables as being explained by the model.) This comes in handy to know when using the rule in the identity problem below. (The identity problem is a GIANT pain in the neck but the model cannot be estimated without going through these hoops.)

This is important because a predetermined variable is one that is contemporaneously uncorrelated with the error term in its equation. Note how this ties up with causality. If Y is caused by X then Y cannot be an independent variable in contemporaneously predicting/explaining Y.

Say we have a system common in economics:

$$Q(\text{demand}) = D(I) + D(\text{price}) + \text{Income} + D(\text{error})$$
$$Q(\text{supply}) = S(I) + S(\text{price}) + S(\text{error})$$

Note that the variables Q and price are endogenous (computed within the system) and income is exogenous. That is, income is given. (D(I) is the intercept in the demand equation and S(I) is the intercept in the supply equation.) These equations are called structural forms of the model. Algebraically, these structural forms can be solved for endogenous variables giving a reduced form of the equations.

> **Reduced form equations:** in econometrics, models solved in terms of endogenous variables.

That is:

$$Q = \left(\frac{D(price) * S(I) - D(I) * S(price)}{D(price) - S(price)}\right) - \left(\frac{Income * S(price)}{D(price) - S(price)}\right) Income$$

$$+ \left(\frac{-S(price) * D(error) + D(price) * S(error)}{D(price) - S(price)}\right)$$

$$P = \left(\frac{-D(I) + S(I)}{D(price) - S(price)}\right) - \left(\frac{Income}{D(price) - S(price)}\right) Income + \left(\frac{-D(error) + S(error)}{D(price) - S(price)}\right)$$

The reduced form of the equations shows how the endogenous variables (those determined within the system) DEPEND on the predetermined variables and error terms. That is, the values of Q and P are explicitly determined by income and errors. This means that income is given to us.

Note that the endogenous variable price appears as an independent variable in each equation. In fact, it is NOT independent, it depends on income and error terms and this is the issue. It is specifically correlated with its own (contemporaneous) error term. Correlation of an independent variable and its error terms leads to inconsistent results.

Why go to the trouble of using simultaneous equations?

First, because it's fun. Also note that if a system should be modelled with simultaneous equations and IS NOT, the parameter estimates are INCONSISTENT! Lastly, insights are more realistic. The simulation suggests the appropriate complexity.

Conceptual basics

Generally, any economic model has to have the number of variables with values to be explained to be equal to the number of independent relationships in the model. This is the identification problem.

Many textbooks (Kmenta, Kennedy, Greene, etc) can give the mathematical derivation for the solution of simultaneous equations. The general problem is that there have to be enough known variables to 'fix' each unknown quantity estimated. That is, there needs to be a rule. The good news is that there is. Here is the rule for solving the identification problem:

> *The number of predetermined variables excluded*
> *in the equation MUST be >= the number of endogenous*
> *variables included in the equation, less one.*

Let's use this rule on the supply–demand equation above:

$$Q(\text{demand}) = D(I) + D(\text{price}) + \text{Income} + D(\text{error})$$
$$Q(\text{supply}) = S(I) + S(\text{price}) + S(\text{error})$$

Demand: the number of predetermined variables excluded = zero. Income is the only predetermined variable and it IS NOT excluded from the demand equation. The number of endogenous variables included less one = 2 – 1 = 1. The two endogenous variables are quantity and price. So the number of predetermined variables excluded in the equation = 0 and this is < the number of endogenous variables included in the equation. Therefore the demand equation is under-identified.

Supply: the number of predetermined variables excluded = one. Income is the only predetermined variable and it is excluded from the supply equation. The number of endogenous variables included less one = 2 – 1 = 1. The two endogenous variables are quantity and price. So the number of predetermined variables excluded in the equation = 0 and this is < the number of endogenous variables included in the equation. Therefore the supply equation is exactly identified.

Desirable properties of estimators

We have not talked about (and it's about time we did) what are the desirable properties of estimators. That is, we have spent effort estimating coefficients on, say, price and advertising but have not discussed how to know if the estimator is 'good'. That is the purpose of the following brief description. If you need a fuller (more theoretically statistical) background virtually any econometrics textbook will suffice. (As mentioned in the introduction to this book, I personally like Kmenta's *Elements of Econometrics* and Kennedy's *A Guide to Econometrics*.)

Unbiasedness

A desirable property most econometricians agree on is unbiasedness. Unbiasedness has to do with the sampling distribution (remember the statistical introduction chapter? You didn't think that would ever be mentioned again, did you?).

If we take an unlimited number of samples of whatever coefficient we're estimating, and average each of these samples together and plot the distribution of those averages of the samples, what we would end up with is the distribution of the beta coefficient of that variable. The average of these averages is the correct value of the beta coefficient, on average. Honest. Now what does this mean? It means the estimator of beta is said to be unbiased if the mean of the (very large number of samples) sampling distribution is the same value as the estimated beta coefficient. That is, if the average value of beta in repeated sampling is beta, then the estimator for beta is unbiased, on average. Note that this does NOT mean that the estimated value of beta is the correct value of beta. It means ON AVERAGE the estimated value of beta will be the value of beta. Sounds like double talk, huh?

The obvious question is how do you know if your estimator is unbiased? That is unfortunately a very mathematically complex discussion. The short answer is: it depends on how the data is generated and it depends a lot on the distribution of the error term of the model. Remember statistics uses inductive thinking (not deductive thinking) so it is viewed from inferences, indirectly. That is, an estimator, say, via regression, is designed with these properties in mind. Thus these properties produce assumptions to take into account how the data is generated and what that does to the disturbance and hence what that means for the sampling distribution. As an example, for regression, the assumptions are:

1 The dependent variable actually DEPENDS on a linear combination of independent variables and coefficients.

2 The average of the error term is zero.

3 The error terms have no serial correlation and have the same variance (with all independent variables).

4 The independent variables are fixed in repeated samples, often called non-stochastic X.

5 There is no perfect collinearity between the independent variables.

In a very real way, econometric modelling is all about dealing with (detecting and correcting) violations of the above assumptions. Just to make the obvious point: these assumptions are made so that the sampling distribution of the parameter estimates have desirable properties, such as unbiasedness. Now, how important is unbiasedness? Some econometricians claim it is VERY important and they spend all their time and effort around that (and other properties). I myself take little comfort in unbiasedness. I want to know if the estimators are biased or not, maybe even a guess as to how much, but in the real world, it is not often of much practical matter. This is because you could have theoretically any number of samples and while on average the sampling distribution IS the real beta estimate, you never really know which sample you have. It's possible you have an unusually bad sample. And in the real world you are not usually able to take many samples, indeed you usually only have ONE, the one in front of you.

Efficiency

What is often more meaningful, after unbiasedness, in many cases, is efficiency. That is, an estimator that has minimum variance of all the unbiased estimators. In simple terms it means that estimator, of all the unbiased estimators, has the smallest variance.

Consistency

Unbiasedness and efficiency are about the sampling distribution of the estimated coefficient and do not depend on the size of the sample. Asymptotic properties are about the sampling distribution of the estimated coefficient in large samples. Consistency is an asymptotic (large sample) property.

Because the sampling distribution changes as the sample size increases, the mean and the variance can change. Consistency is the property that the true beta value will collapse to the point of the population beta value, as sample size increases to infinity.

Consistency is something I like a lot, because (in database marketing, for example) we typically work with very large samples and therefore can take comfort in the sampling properties of the estimators.

Why am I bringing all the above up now? Because in simultaneous equations, the only property the estimators can have (because the independent variables will NOT be fixed in repeated samples, that is, the non-stochastic X assumption is violated) will be consistency.

BUSINESS CASE

Scott's boss called him into his office. The subject of the meeting invite was 'Cannibalization?'

'Scott, our pricing teams are always at war, as you know. We have always felt that one product could cannibalize another with wild pricings from the product teams.'

'Yeah, we talk about that every quarter.'

'What I wondered was, given your success at quantifying so much of our marketing operations, can we do something about cannibalization?'

'What do you mean, "do something about it"?'

'Can we put together some model of optimization? What prices SHOULD the three product teams charge, in order to maximize our overall revenue?'

'So it's pricing for the enterprise instead of pricing for the product. That sounds like a very complicated problem.'

'But it is similar to the elasticity modelling that you did, especially in terms of substitutes, right?'

'Yeah, I think so. I'm not sure how to get the demand of each product into the regression. I'll have to research it.'

'Great, thanks. E-mail me tomorrow with your ideas.'

Scott looked at him and blinked. His boss turned his chair around and went back to looking over his other e-mails. Scott got up and went back to his place, a little bewildered.

Could it be just having a demand equation for, say, desktops that included the price of desktops as well as the prices of notebooks and servers? That did not seem like it took into account all of the information available. That is, there must be cross-equation correlation, meaning consumers feel the prices of notebooks change as they shop for a desktop, etc. What Scott needed was a way to simultaneously model the impact of each product's price on each product's demand.

$$\begin{vmatrix} qDT = pDT + pNB + pWS \\ qNB = pDT + pNB + pWS \\ qWS = pDT + pNB + pWS \end{vmatrix}$$

The above is a demand system. It is a set of three simultaneous equations that are solved (naturally) simultaneously. This set of equations posits that the demand (quantity) of each product is impacted by the own-price of the product as well as the cross-price of the other products.

Note that the approach here will be fairly brief and econometrically oriented. For a detailed mathematical and microeconomically oriented treatment, see Angus Deaton and John Muellbauer's outstanding 1980 work *Economics and Consumer Behavior*. In that book they thoroughly detail consumer demand and demand systems wherein they ultimately posit the (unfortunately named) Almost Ideal Demand System (AIDS).

So Scott researched simultaneous equations. Right away it was obvious that this technique violates the OLS assumption of independent variables fixed in repeated sample, or non-stochastic X. That is, the independent variables solution depended on the values of the independent variables in the other equations. This ultimately meant the only desirable property (not unbiasedness, not efficiency) was consistency. That is, simultaneous equations have desirable asymptotic properties.

Scott found another issue resulting from simultaneous equations: the problem of identity. He had to apply the rule (mentioned above) that each equation be at least just identified. Recall the rule for identification is:

The number of predetermined variables
excluded in the equation be >= the number
of endogenous variables included in the
equation, less one.

Now Scott had to put together the equations from the data he collected. He got weekly data on desktop, notebook and workstation sales (units) for the last three years. He got total revenue of each as well, which would give him average price (price = total revenue / units). He would use seasonality and consumer confidence. He collected number of direct mails sent and the number of e-mails sent, opened and clicked by week.

Scott put together the results below from the model (Table 8.1). Note the identification status on all is 'over identified'. For desktops: the number of predetermined variables excluded is 4 (number of e-mails, number of visits, January and October) and the number of endogenous variables included (less one) is 3 (quantity of desktops, price of desktops, price of notebooks and price of workstations). Thus, 4 > 3. For notebooks: the number of predetermined variables excluded is 4 (number of direct mails, consumer confidence, December and October) and the number of endogenous variables included (less one) is 3 (quantity of notebooks, price of desktops, price of notebooks and price of workstations). Thus, 4 > 3. For workstations: the number of predetermined variables excluded is 6 (number of e-mails, number of direct mails, number of visits, consumer confidence, December and August) and the number of endogenous variables included (less one) is 3 (quantity of workstations, price of desktops, price of notebooks and price of workstations). Thus, 6 > 3.

Table 8.1 Model results

	Price DT	Price NB	Price WS	# DMs	# EMs	# Visits	Cons conf	Jan	Dec	Oct	Aug
Quantity DT	−1.2	2.3	0.4	3.7	XX	XX	5.3	XX	1.2	XX	0.5
Quantity NB	1.1	−2	0.2	XX	6.2	2.2	XX	−0.8	XX	XX	2.9
Quantity WS	0.2	0.8	−2.6	XX	XX	XX	XX	−1.1	XX	−1.9	XX

Now, what does Table 8.1 mean? This was designed as an optimal pricing problem. What does the model tell Scott?

First, since the focus is on pricing and specifically cannibalization, look at the desktop model. The price coefficient is negative, as we'd expect: price goes up, quantity goes down. Now notice the coefficient on notebooks. It's positive (+2.3). This means it is seen (by desktop buyers) as a potential substitute. Note that if notebook prices go down that is positively correlated with the demand for desktops and the quantity of desktops will GO DOWN as well. This is key strategic information. It means the pricing people cannot (and never could) price in a vacuum. Remember Hazlitt's book *Economics in One Lesson* (1979)? The lesson was that everything is (directly or indirectly) connected. What happens with notebook prices affects what happens to desktop demand. This means a portfolio approach should be taken and not a silo approach. Note as well that, in the desktop equation, the prices of workstations are also a substitute, but less. It's obvious that this information can be used to maximize total profit. It might be that one particular brand (or product) will subsidize others, but a successful firm will operate as an enterprise. Similar conclusions are for the other products, in terms of pricing.

The other independent variables are interpreted likewise. Consumer confidence and number of direct mails are positive in influencing desktops sales but not in the other products. For notebooks, e-mails and visits are positive but January seasonality is negative. For workstations both January and October are negative. All of this is strategically lucrative. For example, don't send e-mails to desktops targets, don't send direct mails to notebook targets and don't do much marcom in January.

Scott used the above model to help reorganize the pricing teams. They began to price as an enterpriser and not in silos. Not all of them liked it at first but the increases in revenue (which translated into bonuses for them) helped to assuage their misgivings.

Conclusion

Simultaneous equations can quantify phenomena and can give answers impossible to get otherwise. Yes, it's difficult, requires specialized software and a high level of expertise. But, as the business case above shows, how else would the firm know about optimizing prices across products or brands? In short, the price is worth it.

Checklist

You'll be the smartest person in the room if you:

- ☐ Learn to enjoy the added complexity that simultaneous equations bring to analytics – it better matches consumer behaviour.

- ☐ Remember that simultaneous equations use two kinds of variables: predetermined (lagged endogenous and exogenous) and endogenous variables.

- ☐ Point out that estimators have desirable properties: unbiasedness, efficiency, consistency, etc.

- ☐ Observe that econometrics is really all about detecting and correcting violations of assumptions (linearity, normality, spherical error terms, etc).

- ☐ Prove that simultaneous equations can be used for optimal pricing and understanding cannibalization between products, brands, etc.

PART THREE
Inter-relationship techniques

What does my (customer) market look like?

09

Modelling inter-relationship techniques

Introduction

As mentioned earlier, there are two general types of multivariate analysis: dependent variable techniques and inter-relationship techniques. Most of the first part of this book has been concerned with dependent variable techniques. These include all of the types of regression (ordinary, logistic, survival modelling, etc), as well as discriminate analysis, conjoint analysis, etc.

The point of dependent variable techniques is to understand to what extent the dependent variable depends on the independent variables. That is, how does price impact units, where units is the dependent variable (something we are trying to understand or explain) and price is the independent variable, a variable that is hypothesized to cause the movement in the dependent variable.

Inter-relationship techniques have a completely different point of view. These include multivariate algorithms like factor analysis, segmentation, multi-dimensional scaling, etc. Inter-relationship techniques are trying to understand how variables (price, product purchases, advertising spend, etc) interact (inter-relate) together. Remember how factor analysis was used to correct for collinearity in regression? It did this by extracting the variance of the independent variables in such a way so as each factor (which contained the variables) was uncorrelated with all other factors, that is, the inter-relationship between the independent variables was constructed to form factors.

This section will spend considerable effort on an inter-relationship technique that is of upmost interest and importance to marketing: segmentation.

Introduction to segmentation

Okay. This introductory chapter is designed to detail some of the strategic uses and necessities of segmentation. The chapter following this will dive into more of the analytic techniques and what segmentation output may look like. Segmentation is often the biggest analytic project available and one that provides potentially more strategic insights than any other. Plus, it's fun!

What is segmentation? What is a segment?

A good place to start is to make sure we know what we're talking about. Radical, I know. By definition, segmentation is a process of taxonomy, a way to divide something into parts, a way to separate a market into sub-markets. It can be called things like 'clustering' or 'partitioning'. Thus, a market segment (cluster) is a subset of the market (or customer market, or database, etc),

> **Segmentation:** in marketing strategy, a method of sub-dividing the population into similar sub-markets for better targeting, etc.

The general definition of a segment is that members are 'homogeneous within and heterogeneous between'. That means that a good segmentation solution will have all the members (say, customers) within a segment very similar to each other but very dissimilar to all members of all other segments. Homogeneous means 'same' and heterogeneous means 'different'.

It's possible to have very advanced statistical algorithms to accomplish this, or it can be a very crude business rule. The next chapter will mention a few statistical techniques for doing segmentation. Note that a business rule could simply be, 'Separate the database into four parts: highest use, medium use, low use and no use of our product'. This managerial fiat has been (and still is) used by many companies.

RFM (recency, frequency and monetary variables) is another simple business rule: separate the database into, say, deciles based on three metrics: how recently a customer purchased, how frequently a customer purchased and how much money a customer spent. Many companies are not doing much more than this, in terms of segmentation. These companies are certainly not marketing companies because techniques like RFM are really from a financial, and not a customer, point of view. Therefore, a segment is that entity wherein all members assigned to that segment are, by some definition, alike.

Why segment? Strategic uses of segmentation

So, why segment at all? There are three typical uses of segmentation: finding similar members, making modelling better and – most important – using marketing strategy to attack each segment differently.

Finding homogeneous members is a valuable use of a statistical technique. The business problem tends to be: find all those that are 'alike' and see how, say, satisfaction differs between them, or find all those that are 'homogeneous' by some measure and see how usage varies between them.

A simple example might be in, say, telecommunications, where we are looking at churn (attrition) rates. We want to understand the motivation of churn, what behaviour can predict churn. So, conduct segmentation and identify customers in each segment that are alike in all important ways to the business (products, usage, demographics, channel preferences, etc) and show different churn rates by segment. Note that churn is not the variable that all segments are alike on, churn is what we are trying to understand. Thus we control for several influences (all members within a segment are alike) and now can see high vs low churners, after all other significant variables have been eliminated.

A second usage, also sophisticated and nuanced, is to use segmentation to improve modelling. In the above churn example, say segmentation was done and we want to predict churn. We run a separate regression model for each segment and find that different independent variables affect churn differently.

This will be far more accurate (and actionable) than one (average) model applied to everyone without segmentation. This approach takes advantage of the different reasons to churn. One segment might churn due to dropped calls, another might churn because of the price of the plan and another is sensitive to their bill based on calls, minutes and data used. Thus, each model will exploit these differences and be far more accurate than otherwise. The more accurate the model, the greater the insights; the greater the understanding, the more obvious the strategy of how to combat churn in each segment.

But from a marketing point of view, the reason to segment is the simple answer that not everyone is alike; not all customers are the same. One size does not fit all.

I'd even offer a tweak on 'segmentation' at this point. Market segmentation uses the marketing concept, where the customer is king and strategy is therefore customer-centric. Note that an algorithm like RFM is from the firm's (financial) point of view with metrics that are important to the firm. RFM is about designing value tiers based on a financial perspective (see Chapter 10 highlight, 'Why go beyond RFM?').

Since marketing segmentation should be from the customer's point of view, why do segmentation? That is, how does 'one size does not fit all' operate in terms of customer-centricity?

Generally, it's based on recognizing that different customers have different sensitivities. These different sensitivities cause them to behave differently because they are motivated differently.

This means considerable effort needs to be applied to learn what makes each behavioural segment a segment. (The specific techniques to do this are explained in the next chapter.) It means developing a strategy to exploit these different sensitivities and motivations.

Usually there is a segment sensitive to price, and a segment not sensitive to price. Often there is a segment that prefers one channel (say online) and a segment that prefers another channel (say offline). Typically one segment will have high penetration of product X while another segment will have high penetration of product Y. One segment needs to be communicated to differently (style, imaging, messaging, etc) than another segment. Note that this is far more involved than a simple business rule.

The idea is that if a segment is sensitive to, say, price, then those members should get a discount or a better offer, in order to maximize their probability to purchase (they face an elastic demand curve). The segment that is not sensitive to price (because they are loyal, wealthy, no substitutes available, etc) should not be given the discount because they don't need it in order to purchase.

I know the above adds complexity to the analysis. But note that consumer behaviour IS complex. Behaviour incorporates simultaneous motivations and multi-dimensional factors, sometimes nearly irrational (remember Dan Ariely's book, *Predictably Irrational?*).

Understanding consumer behaviour requires a complex, sophisticated solution, if the goal is to do marketing, if the goal is to be customer-centric. A simpler solution won't work. Much like the problem that happens when we take a three-dimensional globe of the earth and spread it out over a two-dimensional space. Greenland is now way off in size; the world is wrong. Being overly simplistic produces wrong results; just like applying a univariate solution to a multivariate problem will produce wrong results.

For the MBA (which seems to need a list à la PowerPoint) I'd suggest the following as benefits of segmentation:

Marketing Research: learning WHY. Segmentation provides a rationale for behaviour.

Marketing Strategy: targeting by product, price, promotion and place. Strategy uses the marketing mix by exploiting segment differences.

Marketing Communications: messaging and positioning. Some segments need a transactional style of communication; other segments need a relationship style of communication. One size does not fit all.

Marketing Economics: imperfect competition leads to price makers. With the firm communicating just the right product at just the right price in just the right channel at just the right time to the most needy target, such compelling offers give the firm nearly monopolistic power.

The four Ps of strategic marketing

Segmentation is part of a strategic marketing process called the four Ps of strategic marketing, coined by Philip Kotler. Kotler is probably the most widely recognized marketing guru in the world, essentially creating the discipline of marketing as separate from economics and psychology. He wrote many textbooks including *Marketing Management* (1967), now in its 14th edition, which has been used for decades as the pillar of all marketing education.

Most marketers are aware of the four Ps of tactical marketing: product, price, promotion and place. These are often called the 'marketing mix'. But before these are applied, a marketing strategy should be developed, based on the four Ps of strategic marketing.

Partition

The first step is to partition the market by applying a (behavioural) segmentation algorithm to divide the market into sub-markets. This means recognizing strategically that one size does not fit all, and understanding that each segment requires a different treatment to maximize revenue/profit or satisfaction/loyalty.

Probe

This second step is usually about additional data. Often this may come from marketing research, probing for attitudes about the brand, its competitors, shopping and purchasing behaviour, etc. Sometimes it can come from demographic overlay data, which is especially valuable if it includes lifestyle information. Last, probing data can come from created variables from the database itself. These tend to be around velocity (time between purchases) or share of products penetrated (what per cent does the customer buy of category X, what per cent of category Y, etc), seasonality, consumer confidence and inflation, etc.

Prioritize

This step is a financial analysis of the resulting segments. Which are most profitable, which are growing fastest, which require more effort to keep or cost to serve, etc? Part of the point of this step is to find those that we might decide to DE-market, that is, those that are not worth the effort to communicate to.

Position

Positioning is about using all of the above insights and applying an appropriate message, or the correct look and feel and style. This is the tool that allows the creation of compelling messages based on a segment's specific sensitivities. This marketing communication is often called marcom. This incorporates the four Ps of tactical marketing.

Criteria for actionable segmentation

I've always thought the list below guided a segmentation project that ended up being actionable. This too probably came from Philip Kotler (as do most things that are good and important in modern marketing).

Identifiability. In order to be actionable each segment has to be identifiable. Often this is the process of scoring the database with each customer having a probability of belonging to each segment.

Substantiality. Each segment needs to be substantial enough (large enough) to make marketing to it worthwhile. Thus there's a balance between distinctiveness and size.

Accessibility. Not only do the members of the segment have to be identifiable, they have to be accessible. That is, there has to be a way to get to them in terms of marketing efforts. This typically requires having contact info, e-mail, direct mail, SMS, etc.

Stability. Segment membership should not change drastically. The things that define the segments should be stable so that marketing strategy is predictable over time. Segmentation assumes there will be no drastic shocks in demand, or radical changes in technology, etc, in the foreseeable future.

Responsiveness. To be actionable, the segmentation must drive responses. If marcom data is one of the segmentation dimensions, this is usually achievable.

A priori or not?

As this is a practitioner's guide to marketing science, it should come as no surprise that I advocate statistical analysis to perform segmentation. However, it's a fact that sometimes there are (top-down) dictums that define segments. These are managerial fiats that demand a market be based (a priori) on managerial judgement, rather than some analytic technique. The usual dimension(s) managers want to artificially define their market by tend to be usage, profit, satisfaction, size, growth, etc. Analytically, this is a univariate approach to what is clearly a multivariate problem.

In my opinion, there is a place for managerial judgement, but it is NOT in segment definition. After the segments are defined, then managerial judgement should ascertain if the solution makes sense, if the segments themselves are actionable.

Conceptual process

Settle on a (marketing/customer) strategy

The general first step in behavioural segmentation is one of strategy. After the firm establishes goals, a strategy needs to be in place to reach those goals. There should be a champion, a business leader, a stakeholder that is the ultimate user of the segmentation.

Analytics needs to recognize that a segmentation not driven by strategy is akin to a body without a skeleton. Strategy supports everything. A very different segmentation should result if the strategy is about market share as opposed to a strategy about net margin.

A strategy discussion should revolve around customer behaviour. What is the customer's mindset? What is the behaviour we are trying to understand? What incentive are we employing? Any good segmentation solution should tie together customer behaviour and marketing strategy. Remember, marketing is customer-centric.

Collect appropriate (behavioural) data

The next analytic step in behavioural segmentation is to collect appropriate (behavioural) data. This tends to be generally around transactions (purchases) and marcom responses.

A few comments ought to be made about what is meant by 'behavioural data'. My theory of consumer behaviour (and it's okay if you don't agree) is to envision four levels (see Figure 9.1): primary motivations, experiential motivations, behaviours and results. Results (typically financial) are caused by behaviours (usually some kind of transaction purchases and marcom responses), which are caused by one or both (primary and experiential) motivations. Primary motivations (price valuation, attitudes about lifestyle, tastes and preferences, etc) are generally psychographic and not really seen. They are motivational causes (searching, need arousal, etc) without brand interaction. Experiential motivations tend to have brand interaction and are another motivator to additional behaviours that ultimately cause (financial) results. These motivations are things like loyalty, engagement, satisfaction, etc. Note that engagement is an experiential cause (there has

Figure 9.1 Levels of consumer behaviour

been interaction with the brand) and is not a behaviour. Engagement would be metrics like recency and frequency. There will be more on this topic when we discuss RFM (see Chapter 10 highlight). I'll warn you this is one of my soap boxes.

Usually transactions and marcom responses (from direct mail, e-mail, etc) are the main dimensions of behavioural segmentation. Often additional variables are created from these dimensions.

We want to know how many times a customer purchased, how much each time, what products were purchased, what categories each product purchased belonged to, etc. Often valuable profiling variables go along with this, including net margin on each purchase, cost of goods sold, etc. We want to know the number of transactions over a period of time, the number of units and if any discounts were applied to these transactions.

In terms of marcom responses we want to collect what kind of vehicle (direct mail, e-mail, etc), opens, clicks, website visits, store purchases, discounts used, etc. We want to know when each vehicle was sent and what category of product was featured on each vehicle. Any versioning needs to be collected, and any offers/promotions, etc, need to be annotated in the database. All of this data surrounding transactions and responses is the basis of customer behaviour.

Generally we expect to find a segment that is heavily penetrated in one type of category (broad products purchased) but not another and this will be different by more than one segment. As bears repeating, one segment is heavily penetrated by category X, while another is heavily penetrated by category Y, etc. We also expect to find one or more segments that prefer e-mail or online but not direct mail, or vice versa. We typically find a segment that is sensitive to price and one that is not sensitive to price. These insights come differently from these behavioural dimensions.

Create/use additional data

Now comes the fun part. Here you can create additional data. This data at least takes the form of seasonality variables, calculates time between each purchase, time between categories purchased, peaks and valleys of transactions and units and revenue, share of categories (per cent of baby products compared to total, per cent of entertainment categories compared to total), etc. There should be metrics like number of units and transactions per customer, per cent of discounts per customer, top two or three categories purchased per customer, etc. All of these can be used/tested in the segmentation.

As for marcom, there should be a host of metrics around marcom type and offer and time until purchase. There should be business rules tying a campaign to a purchase. There should be variables indicating categories featured on the cover, or subject lines, or offers and promotions.

Note how all of the above expand behavioural data. But there are other sources of data as well. Often primary marketing research is used. This tends to be around satisfaction or loyalty, something about competitive substitutes, maybe marcom awareness or importance of each marcom vehicle.

Third-party overlay data is a rich source of additional insights into fleshing out the segments. This is often matched data like demographics, interests, attitudes, lifestyles, etc. This data is typically most helpful when it deals with attitudes or lifestyle, but demographics can be interesting as well. Again all of this additional data is about fleshing out the segments and trying to understand the mindset/rationale of each segment.

Run the algorithm

As mentioned, the algorithm discussion will be covered in depth in the next chapter, but a few comments can be made now, particularly in terms of process. Note that the algorithm is guided by strategy and uses (defining or segmenting) variables based on strategy.

The algorithm is the analytic guts of segmentation and care should be taken in choosing which technique to use. The algorithm should be fast and non-arbitrary. Analytically, we are trying to achieve maximum separation (segment distinctiveness).

The ultimate idea of segmentation is to level a different strategy against each segment. Therefore each segment should have a different reason for BEING a segment. The algorithm needs to provide diagnostics to guide optimization. The general metric of success is 'homogeneous within and heterogeneous between' segments. There have been many such metrics offered (SAS, via proc discrim, uses 'the logarithm of the determinant of the covariance matrix' as a metric of success). In the profiling, the differentiation of each segment should make itself clear.

Just to stack the deck, let me define what a good algorithm for segmentation should be. It should be multivariable, multivariate and probabilistic. It should be multivariable because consumer behaviour is most certainly explained by more than one variable, and it should be multivariate because these variables are impacting consumer behaviour simultaneously, interacting with each other. It should be probabilistic because consumer behaviour is probabilistic; it has a distribution and at some point that behaviour can even be irrational. Gasp!

Profile the output

Profiling is what we show to other people to prove that the solution does discriminate between segments. Generally the means and/or frequencies of each key variable (especially transactions and marcom responses) are shown to quickly gauge differences by each segment. Note that the more distinct each segment is the more obvious a strategy (for each segment) becomes.

To show the means of KPIs (key performance indicators) by segment is common, but often another metric teases out differences better. Using indexes often speeds distinctiveness. That is, take each segment's mean and divide by the total mean. For example, say segment one has average revenue of 1,500 and segment two has average revenue of 750 and the total average (all segments together) is 1,000. Dividing segment one by the total is 1,500/1,000 = 1.5, that is, segment one has revenue 50% above average. Note also that segment two is 750/1,000 = 0.75 meaning that segment two contributes revenue 25% less than average. Applying indexes to all metrics by segment immediately shows differences. This is especially obvious where small numbers are concerned. As another example, say segment one has a response rate of 1.9% and the overall grand total response rate is 1.5%. While these numbers (segment one to total) are only 0.4% different, note that the index of segment one/total is 1.9%/1.5% showing that segment one is 27% greater than average. This is why we like to (and should) use indexes.

While seeing drastic differences in each segment is very satisfying, the most enjoyable part of profiling often is the NAMING of each segment. First you must realize that naming a segment helps distinguish the segments. The more segments you have the more important this becomes.

I have a couple of suggestions about naming segments; take them as you see fit. Sometimes the naming of segments is left to the creative department and that's okay. But usually analytics has to come up with names.

Each name should be only two or three words, if possible. They should be more informative than something like 'High Revenue Segment' or 'Low Response Segment'. They should incorporate two or three similar dimensions. Either keep most of them to product marcom response dimensions, or keep them along a strategic dimension or two (high growth, cost to serve, net margin, etc). It's tempting to name them playfully but this still has to be usable. That is, while 'Bohemian Mix' is fun, what does it mean strategically or from a marketing point of view?

Model to score database (if from a sample)

The next step, if the segmentation was done on a sample, is to score the database with each customer's probability to belong to each segment. This is often carried out quickly with discriminate analysis. Apply (in SAS) proc discrim to the sample and get the equations that score each customer into a segment. (Discriminate analysis is a common technique, once categories (segments) are defined, to fit variables in equations to predict category (segment) membership.) Then run these equations against the database.

If this is accurate enough (whatever 'accurate enough' means) then you're good to go. But discrim sometimes is NOT accurate enough. I myself think this is because you have to use the same variables (although with different weights) on each segment. This can be inefficient. There is also the assumption inherent in proc discrim about the same variance across a segment, which is hardly ever true, so you may need to turn to another technique.

I have often settled for logistic regression, where a different equation scores each segment. That is, if I have five segments, the first logit will be with a binary dependent variable: 1 if the customer is in segment one and 0 if not. The second logit will be a 1 if the customer is in segment two and a 0 if not. Then I put in variables to maximize probability of each segment and I remove those variables that are insignificant and run all equations against all customers. Each customer will have a probability to belong to each segment and the maximum score wins, ie, the segment that has the highest probability is the segment to which the customer is assigned.

Test and learn

The typical last step is to create a test and learn plan. This is generally a broad-based test design, aimed at learning which elements drive results, which is directly informed by the segmentation insights.

Note Chapter 11 on design of experiments (DOE). The overall idea here is to develop a testing plan to take advantage of segmentation. The first thing to test is typically selection/targeting. That is, pull a sample of those likely to belong to a very highly profitable heavy usage segment and do a mailing to them, and compare revenue and responses to some general control group. These high-end segments should drastically out-perform the business as usual (BAU) group.

A common next step (depending on strategy, etc) might be promotional testing. This would usually follow with elasticity modelling by segment. Often one or more segments are found to be insensitive to price and one or more segments are found to be sensitive to price. The test here is to offer promotions and determine if the segment insensitive to price will still purchase even with a lower discount. This means the firm does not have to give away margin to get the same amount of purchases.

Other typical tests revolve around product categories, channel preference and messaging. A full factorial design could generate many insights immediately and then marcom could be aimed appropriately. The general idea is that if a segment is, say, heavily penetrated in product X, send them a product X message. If a segment might have a propensity for product Y (given product X) do a test and see how to incentivize broader category purchases. The next chapter will go through a detailed example of what this testing might mean.

Checklist

You'll be the smartest person in the room if you:

- ☐ Point out that segmentation is a strategic, not an analytic, exercise.

- ☐ Remember that segmentation is mostly a marketing construct.

- ☐ Argue that segmentation is about what's important to a consumer, not what's important to a firm.

- ☐ Recall that segmentation gives insights into marketing research, marketing strategy, marketing communications and marketing economics.

- ☐ Observe the four Ps of strategic marketing: partition, probe, prioritize and position.

- ☐ Uncompromisingly demand that RFM be viewed as a service to the firm, not a service to the consumer.

- ☐ Require each segment to have its own story rationale for why it is a segment. There should be a different strategy levelled at each segment, otherwise there is no point in it being a segment.

Segmentation   10

Tools and techniques

Overview

The previous chapter was meant to be a general/strategic overview of segmentation. This chapter is designed to show the analytic aspects of it, which is the heart of the segmentation process. Analytics is the fulcrum of the whole project.

A few books to note, in terms of the analytics of segmentation, would be *Segmentation and Positioning for Strategic Marketing Decisions* by James H Myers (1996), *Market Segmentation* by Michel Wedel and Wagner A Kamakura (1998) and *Advanced Methods of Marketing Research*, edited by Richard P Bagozzi (1994), especially the chapters 'The CHAID Approach to Segmentation Modeling' and 'Cluster Analysis in Market Research'. Note also the papers of Jay Magdison (2002) from the *Statistical Innovations* website (www.statisticalinnovations.com).

Metrics of successful segmentation

As mentioned earlier, the general idea of successful segmentation is 'homo-geneous within and heterogeneous between'. There are several possible approaches to quantifying this goal. Generally, a ratio of those members in the segment is compared to all those members not in the segment, and the smaller the better. This helps us to compare a three-segment solution with a four-segment solution, or a four-segment solution using variables a–f with a four-segment solution using variables d–j. SAS (via proc discrim) has the 'log of the determinant of the covariant matrix'. This is a good metric to use in comparing solutions even if it's a badly-named one.

General analytic techniques

Business rules

There may be a place for business-rule segmentation. If data is sparse, under populated, or very few dimensions are available, there's little point trying to do an analytic segmentation. There's nothing for the algorithm to operate on.

I (again) caution against a managerial fiat. I have had managers who invested themselves in the segmentation design. They have told me how to define the segments. This is typically flawed. I wouldn't say to ignore manage-ment's knowledge/intuition of their market and their customers. My advice is to go through the segmentation process, do the analytics and see what the results look like. Typically the analytic results are appealing and more compelling than managerial judgement. This is because a manager's dictum is around one or two or at most three dimensions, arbitrarily defined. But the analytic output optimizes the variables and separation is the mathemati-cal 'best'. It would be unlikely that one person's intuition could out-perform a statistical algorithm. I would even say that if an analytic output is very different than a manager's point of view, that manager has a lot to learn about his own market. The statistical algorithm encourages learning. Most often managerial fiat is about usage (high, medium and low), satisfaction, net profit, etc. None of these require/allow much investigation into WHY the results are what they are. None of these require an understanding of consumer behaviour.

This is why RFM (recency, frequency, and monetary) is so insidious. It is a business rule, it's appealing, it is based on data and it works. It is ultimately a (typically financial) manager's point of view. It does not encourage learning.

Marketing strategy is reduced to nothing more than migrating lower value tiers into higher value tiers.

A good overview of segmentation, from the managerial role and not the analytical role, is Art Weinstein's book, *Market Segmentation* (1994), which provides a good discussion of segmentation based on business rules.

CHAID

CHAID (chi-squared automatic interaction detection) is an improvement over AID (automatic interaction detection). Strictly speaking, CHAID is a dependent variable technique, NOT an inter-relationship technique. I'm including it here because CHAID is often used as a segmentation solution.

This brings us to the first question: 'Why use a dependent variable technique in terms of segmentation?' My answer is that it is inappropriate. A dependent variable technique is designed to understand (predict) what causes a dependent variable to move. By definition, segmentation is not about explaining the movement in some dependent variable.

Okay. How does it work? While there are many variations of the algorithm, in general it works the following way. CHAID takes the dependent variable, looks at the independent variables and finds the one independent variable that 'splits' the dependent variable best. 'Best' here is per the chi-squared test. (AID was based on the F-test, which is the ratio of explained variance over unexplained variance and is used (in modelling) as a threshold that proves the model is better than random.) It then takes that (second level) variable and searches the remaining independent variables to test which one best splits that second level variable. It does this until the number of levels assigned is reached, or until there is no improvement in convergence.

Below is a simple example (Figure 10.1). Product revenue is the dependent variable and CHAID is run and the best split is found to be income. Income is split into two groups: high income and low income. The next best variable is response rate, where each income level has two different response rates. High income is split in terms of response rate > 9% and response rate > 6% and < 9%. Low income is split between < 2% and > 2% and < 6%. Thus this simplified example would show four segments: high income high response, high income medium response, low income medium response and low income low response.

The advantages of CHAID are that it is simple, easy to use and easy to explain. It provides a stunning visual to show how to interpret its output.

The disadvantages are many. First, it is not a model in the statistical/mathematical sense of the word, but a heuristic, a guide. This means the

Figure 10.1   CHAID output

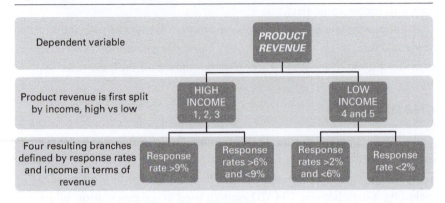

analysis tends to be unstable; that is, different samples can produce wildly different results. There are no coefficients that show significance, there are no signs on the variables (positive or negative) and there is no real measure of fit.

CHAID is a popular technique, due to its ease and simplicity. I would offer it is not appropriate for segmentation. Its best use is probably in terms of data exploration. I would caution, however, that this can become a crutch and might encourage you to bypass your own brain. I remember when someone who worked for me was assigned to build a regression model. She had CHAID on her PC so she was running all kinds of CHAID output and had many pages of tree diagrams. After a while I asked how it was going and she was still exploring the data. She had hundreds of variables and she said she had no real idea about what caused what. She claimed she needed CHAID to mine the data because she had no clue what variables might cause/explain the movement in the dependent variable. I told her that if she, as the analyst, truly had no idea whatsoever as to what might cause or explain the movement in the dependent variable (in this case sales) then she was not the right person to do the model. As analyst you MUST have some idea of the data-generating process and you MUST have some idea about 'this causes that', eg, price changes cause changes in demand. So, use CHAID for designing structure, not explaining causality.

Hierarchical clustering

Hierarchical clustering IS an inter-relationship technique. It also has a graphical display but unlike CHAID it is NOT visually appealing.

Hierarchical clustering calculates a 'nearness metric', a type of similarity via some inter-relationship variables. There are many options for how to do this but conceptually the idea is that some observations (say customers) are 'close to each other' based on some similar variables. Then a dendogram (a horizontal tree structure) is produced and the analyst chooses how to divide the resultant graphics. See Figure 10.2.

Note that, for instance, observations 34 and 56 are joined together (because they are similar) and these are next joined to observation 111. Now there are three observations in this cluster. As the number of observations increases the graphic is less and less usable. One disadvantage is that the analyst is required to (arbitrarily) decide where to break the clusters off. That is, it ultimately is up to the analyst to choose how many and which observations are in the final clusters. Arbitrary choice is NOT based on analytics, but intuition.

An advantage of hierarchical clustering is it calculates the distance of every observation from all other observations, so the starting 'seeds' are mathematically distinct. Often hierarchical clustering is used for nothing other than these starting seeds as an input into another algorithm. Note well James H Myers' book on segmentation (Myers, 1996), which has a very good and conceptual treatment of hierarchical clustering.

K-means clustering

K-means is probably the most popular (analytic) segmentation technique. SAS (using proc fastclus) and SPSS (using partitioning) have very powerful algorithms to do K-means clustering. K-means is easy to do, fairly easy to understand and explain and the output is compelling. K-means works and has been in use for over 50 years.

K-means was invented by zoologists in the 1960s for phylum classification. While EW Forgy, RC Jancey and MR Anderberg were early algorithm designers (1960s) it was James MacQueen (1967) who coined the term 'K-means'. It's called K-means because K is the number of clusters and the centroids are the means of the clusters. Note they were trying to decide, based on an animal's (particularly a butterfly's) characteristics, to which phylum they belonged. They wanted an algorithm for taxonomy.

The general algorithm (and as with all other techniques, there are various versions) is as follows:

1 Set up: choose number of clusters, choose some kind of 'maximum distance' to define cluster membership and choose which clustering variables to use.

Figure 10.2   Hierarchical clustering – dendogram

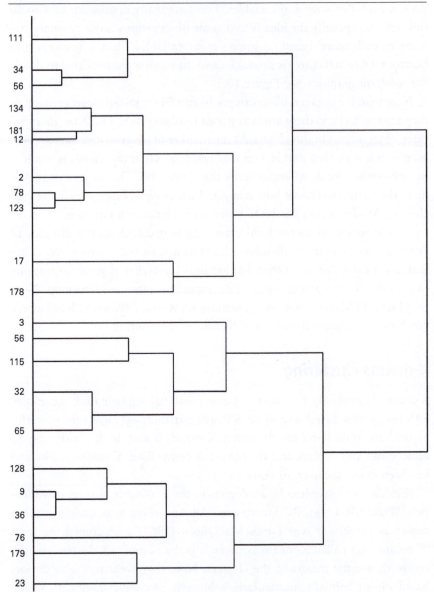

2 Find the first observation that has all the clustering variables populated and call this cluster 1.

3 Find the next observation that has all the clustering variables populated and test how far away this observation is from the first observation. If it's far enough away then call this cluster 2.

4 Find the next observation that has all the clustering variables populated and test how far away this observation is from the first and second observations (clusters). If it's far enough away then call this cluster 3. Continue with steps 2–4 until the number of clusters chosen is defined.

5 Go to the next observation and test which cluster it is closest to and assign that observation to that cluster.

6 Continue with step 5 until all observations that have the clustering variables populated have been assigned.

There are several things good about this algorithm. It is very fast and can handle a large amount of data. It works. It will achieve some kind of separation.

There are many disadvantages. Personally, I HATE the arbitrariness of what the analyst must decide. As stated above, the analyst tells the algorithm how many clusters to form (as if he knows). There is little (analytically) to base this important criterion on. Second, he has to tell the algorithm what variables to use to define the clusters. Again, as if he knows how many clusters there are. This is an extremely important choice. The clusters are DEFINED based on this arbitrary choice.

Another disadvantage with K-means is that there are no real diagnostics on how well it fits, how well it predicts and how well it scores those observations (customers) into each segment. Because it's based on the square root of Euclidean distance

$$\sqrt{\frac{X2 - X1}{Y2 - Y1}}$$

each observation is placed in the segment it is 'closest to'. There is no likelihood metric. Suppose a customer is new on file, or has some unusual behaviour. This customer might not exhibit real segment behaviour but is placed somewhere, regardless.

Because of these arbitrary choices (and the fact that K-means gives no diagnostics to aid these choices) most clustering projects end up with the analyst generating many solutions. He will do a four and a five and a six and a seven and an eight-cluster solution. He will use in each variables 1–5 and then variables 5–10 and then variables 10–12, etc. Because there are no real diagnostics to guide him he will output reams of paper and share these piles of profiles with his peers and the ultimate users of the segmentation and basically throw up his hands and say, 'What do you think? Which of these 20 outputs do you like the best?' And then maybe somebody will decide what they like, typically for strategic reasons. Note the subjectivity here?

Another obvious disadvantage (given the algorithm above) is that if the order of the dataset is different, the K-means solution will be different. Some algorithms improve this option by not just going down the list, but taking a random observation as each starting seed. This is better, but the same problem remains. Re-order, or re-do, the algorithm – with the same number of clusters and the same variables – and the output will be (very) different. This should strike all analytic people as a great problem.

A last problem with K-means is that it is not an optimizing algorithm. It does not try to maximize/minimize anything. It has no generally controlling objective.

Therefore, I would suggest that K-means is not a viable option for actionable segmentation. The algorithm is too arbitrary and the output is subjective, something most good analysts abhor.

Latent class analysis

Latent class analysis (LCA) is a massive improvement on all the above. It is now the state of the art in segmentation. To me, the best software for this is Latent Gold from Statistical Innovations. Jay Magdison is a genius and has written some of the best articles on it. Especially see 'A nontechnical introduction to latent class models' (2002) and 'Latent class models for clustering: a comparison with K-means' (2002).

LCA takes a completely different view of segmentation. Rather than, as in the case of K-means, where the variables define the segments, LCA assumes the scores on the variables are caused by the (hidden) segment. That is, LCA posits a latent (categorical) variable (segment membership) that maximizes the likelihood of observing the scores seen on the variables.

It then runs this taxonomy and creates a probability of each observation belonging to each segment. The segment that has the highest probability is the segment into which the observation is placed. This means LCA is a statistical technique and not a mathematical (like hierarchical or K-means clustering) technique.

There are some disadvantages of LCA. SAS does not do it, at least not as a proc. SPSS does not do it either: you have to buy special software. Statistical Innovations created Latent Gold, which has probably become the gold standard (get it, 'gold'?). It also requires some training and some expertise, but Latent Gold is menu driven and very easy to use. Also, like the light bulb, it is not true that you have to understand all of the intricate details in order to use it. Some training is required, but the results are well worth it.

The advantages have been alluded to but just to be clear, LCA has a LOT of advantages (see Table 10.1). Ultimately segmentation's usefulness is about strategy. The better the distinctiveness the more obviously a strategy becomes levelled on each segment.

However, there are several important analytic advantages, especially in the way Latent Gold articulates the algorithm. First, LCA tells you the optimal number of segments. You do not have to guess. LCA uses the BIC (Bayes Information Criterion) and –LL (negative log likelihood) and error rate to give you diagnostics as to what is the 'best' number of segments given these scores on these variables and this dataset.

Second, LCA gives indications as to which variables are significant in the segmentation solution. You do not have to guess. Any variable that has an $R^2 < 10\%$ can be deemed insignificant.

Third, LCA produces an output that scores every observation with the probability of belonging to each segment. If observation #1 has a probability of belonging to segment 1 of 95% and probability of belonging to segment 2 of 5% it's pretty obvious to which segment that observation belongs. Observation #1 exhibits very strong segment 1 behaviour. But what about observation #2 that has a probability of belonging to segment 1 of 55% and probability of belonging to segment 2 of 45%? This observation does not demonstrate very strong segment behaviour, for any segment. Under K-means this observation would likely be assigned to segment 1. But LCA gives you a diagnostic. Typically some assumption should be made. It's usually something like, any observation that does not score at least 70% likelihood of belonging to any segment should be eliminated from the output. Those observations are placed in some other bucket to be dealt with in some other way. There should not be more than 5% of these outliers, given most marketing models are at 95% confidence. A good solution will have far less than 5% outliers.

These diagnostics make the analytics very fast and very clean. They also make the segmentation solution very distinct. As mentioned, this is the hallmark of a good segmentation solution: distinctiveness. But this is not just valuable for the analyst; it is of utmost importance to the strategist. The more distinct the segmentation solution the clearer each strategy becomes.

Table 10.1 Segmenting algorithms compared

	RFM	CHAID	K-means	LCA
Multivariable	XX	XX	XX	XX
Customer-centric				XX
Multivariate			XX	XX
Probabilistic				XX

BUSINESS CASE

Scott's boss called him into the office. He looked around while his boss played with the phone, which always irritated Scott.

'So Scott', his boss said, grudgingly looking up from his smart phone. 'We are ready to make a major push in consumer strategy. We've added consumer electronics to our product mix and now want to dive deeper.'

'That sounds good. What does that mean for my group?'

'We'd like to explore versioning our direct mail catalogues, positioning our e-mails more strategically, etc. We all remember your ONE SIZE DOES NOT FIT ALL speech at the offsite last quarter.'

'Yeah, sorry, there had been a few cocktails and...'

'No, it's right on. We're talking about initiating a customer market segmentation project and you are slated to lead it.'

Scott gulped. That would be a lot of work. It would be a lot of fun and very visible. 'I'll start putting a team together and begin to go through the process.'

Scott went back to his office (he'd been promoted by now) and sketched out a process, outputting a segmentation based on consumer behaviour. He wrote on his whiteboard a list of steps and then invited stakeholders to a collection of meetings. They were starting a big project: customer segmentation.

Strategize

The first step in behavioural segmentation is to strategize. This tends to be a view from two lenses: marketing strategy and consumer behaviour. These two should not be contradictory.

Scott's team met and there was some discussion but Scott provided leadership on goals based on the mantra of Peter Drucker, the legendary management guru who created business management as a distinct and separate discipline. Drucker said there are only three metrics that make any business sense: increasing revenue, increasing customer satisfaction and decreasing expenses. If you are working on a project that cannot tie to at least one of these metrics you should ask yourself whether you really should be doing that project. Scott's team decided their marketing strategy for the segmentation would be increasing net profit margin. The whole point for each segment was strategizing cross-sell/up-sell opportunities. This was a departure from last year's strategy of mostly acquiring customers. They realized how expensive acquisition can be.

In terms of consumer behaviour, Scott's team hypothesized potential consumer segments. There would likely be one or more generally sensitive to price, one or more having different product penetrations, one or more reacting to compelling messages designed for them and one or more that prefer one channel over another. This is just using tactical marketing (product, price, promotion and place) differentially against each segment.

The real issue was in terms of behaviour. They talked long about what caused the behaviours they would see. They rationalized there might be a consumer segment heavily into games and entertainment, or another consumer segment of very high tech/web-centric/early adopters, etc. There might be another segment needing a relationship, more on the low-tech side, needing their hands held through the techno-babble. They knew most of their (behavioural) data would be transactions and marcom responses.

So the team thought that, given the marketing strategy of increasing net revenue and the various potential consumer behaviour segments, a strategy could be levelled differently at each segment. That is, a completely different com-munication style would be used on, say, a price-sensitive, low-tech consumer as opposed to a heavy gamer. Scott thought there was a lot of excitement and buy-in for this output.

Collect behavioural data

Scott went to his database team and they talked about what data they had. First they had to define a consumer (as opposed to a small business, eg, a sole proprietorship) but that was fairly straightforward. Then they talked about data.

Scott wanted behavioural data, specifically transactions and marcom responses. They talked about two or three years of history. The PC consumer business has a strong seasonality (peaking in August and even more in December) and Scott had already learned how seasonality had to be taken into account.

In terms of transactions, the issue was what kind of granularity was needed. They decided they needed only broad product categories – laptops, desktops and workstations (very few consumers would buy a server) – and only go one level below this, eg, high-end desktop vs scaled-back desktop, and so on. They'd add consumer electronics, which included televisions, printers, software (personal productivity, games, etc), digital cameras, accessories, etc. They'd include pro-duct details as well as gross revenue and discounts applied, net revenue, number of purchases, time between purchases, months the product(s) were purchased, etc.

Thinking about marcom responses (a sign of behaviour and an indication of engagement) they talked about both direct mail and e-mail. They would mostly ignore social media/in-bound marketing because of difficulty in matching customers, and web banner/advertising (again, it cannot be tied directly to a particular customer). They knew to whom they sent a catalogue, when they sent it, what was on the cover and what offers/promotions were inside each one. Each catalogue had a unique 800 phone number, so when the customers rang, the call centre would know which catalogue had driven (at least) that inquiry. If a promotion was used online those were also unique to each catalogue. The same data was available for e-mail. Each was sent to a particular e-mail address and they could keep track of each open and click, etc. So again, there was a lot of data.

Collect additional data

The next step was to collect additional data. This could come from several possible sources. It could come from creating/deriving data from the database. It could come from overlay data and from primary market research data.

From the consumer database they created additional variables. These included monthly dummy variables for seasonality. They calculated time between purchases, they derived typical market baskets and they put together share of products, that is, per cent of desktops, per cent of consumer electronics, and so on.

They purchased overlay data. This included both demographics (such as age, education, income, gender, size of household and occupation) as well as lifestyle and interest variables. They hoped these would flesh out the segments. This data was pretty well matched, at about 80%, to their consumer database.

There was a limited amount of primary marketing research but Scott found a few studies that could be helpful (especially in the probe phase of the four Ps of strategic marketing). They had done a customer satisfaction study and an awareness study. These studies each took customer names from the database and, while not well represented could be matched to the transaction file.

Analytics

Collect data and sample

Note there are two kinds of variables in this environment: segmenting variables and profiling variables. Segmenting variables are those used to create the segments, while profiling variables are everything else. The primary marketing research data will be profiling variables, as they are too under populated to be used as segmenting variables. Most of the demographics will be profiling variables, as demographics are typically not useful in defining segments. But the other (behavioural) variables will go through the algorithm and be tested as to whether or not they are significant and if so will be kept as segmenting variables. Note that anything that is not a segmenting variable will be a profiling variable.

What's next is what Scott has been most looking forward to: the analytics. There are several steps in this process and they are all enjoyable.

So first he would have to take a sample. LCA cannot operate on millions (or even hundreds of thousands) of records. The algorithm would take years to converge. So he chooses a random sample of, say, 20,000 customer records. These records have been matched with transactions and marcom responses, derived data and overlay data and (where possible) primary marketing research data.

Usually there is no need to worry about over sampling (a certain variable) or stratifying, etc.

> **Over sampling:** a sampling technique forcing a particular metric to be over represented (larger) in the sample than in simple random sampling. This is done because a simple random sample would produce too few of that particular metric.

> **Stratifying:** a sampling technique choosing observations based on the distribution of another metric. This is done to ensure the sample contains adequate observations of that particular metric.

In typical consumer marketing a simple random sample is fine. Take a look at any good general statistics book for sampling, etc, such as *Statistical Analysis for Decision Making*, by Morris Hamburg (1987).

Normalize

Now, even though not strictly necessary, is the time to weed out non-normality. I like to do this step to ensure against strange or weird data elements. So, there are two stages.

The first stage is simply to test every variable for 'non-normality'. This generally means taking the z-score of each variable or standardizing each variable, then deleting any observation that has a score > +/– 3.0 standard deviations. (Three standard deviations is 99.9% of the observations in a normal distribution and is therefore very NON-normal.) These are clearly non-normal data elements and there should not be very many of them. Some people replace these outliers with the mean but if there are enough observations this is not necessary and a little too arbitrary for my taste.

For the second stage I will have to ask you to make sure you're sitting down. Remember how I've clamoured about how bad K-means is and how it's not a good solution? Well now I'm asking you to use K-means to test for normality.

The idea is to run K-means with a LOT of clusters, like 100 or so. Use the (typically behavioural) variables that make most sense to you in defining the clusters. All we are trying to do is form clusters that are unusual in terms of behavioural motivations. So now with, say, 100 clusters, those clusters that are very small (like having only a few customers in them) are by multivariate definition 'unusual'. These observations should be eliminated. The point is that while we've looked at any single variable being unusual, this technique uses a multivariable approach to find a group of customers moving in such a way to be non-normal. That's why these observations (customers) are deleted from further analysis.

Note that we are trying to understand the normal market. That's why there is effort put forth to detect non-normality. Because we have a sample it's even more important to ascertain unusual scores on variables or unusual customer behaviour and eliminate it.

So, let's say that Scott and his team did the above process and their sample went from 20,000 to 18,000. Then he randomly splits this 18,000 into two files, A and B. This will be a test file and a validation file for later.

Run LCA

Now Scott feeds test file A into the software and is ready to run LCA. He first chooses to run a solution creating segments 2 through 9, just to narrow down where things are. LCA shows diagnostics (BIC, LL, etc, see above) to help with the optimal number of segments (see Table 10.2). Note that the BIC goes down and is at a minimum at six segments. This tells Scott six segments are probably the right number. The BIC is the Bayes Information Criterion. Think of it as an area of error (essentially negative probability) with the smaller the area the better. Whichever cluster has the smallest error (in terms of predicting membership) the better it is.

Table 10.2 Bayes Information Criterion

	BIC
2 cluster	92,454
3 cluster	79,546
4 cluster	61,565
5 cluster	59,605
6 cluster	**58,456**
7 cluster	58,989
8 cluster	59,650
9 cluster	60,056

Now he runs the second model, after deleting those variables that are insignificant and comes up with Table 10.3.

Table 10.3   Bayes Information Criterion: second model

	BIC
3 cluster	64,466
4 cluster	56,550
5 cluster	41,058
6 cluster	**40,611**
7 cluster	57,089
8 cluster	58,067

The variables he uses also give diagnostics as to which are significant. Note Table 10.4 below, showing $R^2 < 10\%$ for most of the demographics. These Scott removes.

Table 10.4   List of variables removed

Age	0.05
Education (years)	0.07
Income	0.01
Size household	0.02
Occupation – blue collar	0.05
Occupation – white collar	0.04
Occupation – agriculture	0.02
Occupation – government	0.01
Occupation – unemployed	0.02
Ethnicity – asian	0.02
Ethnicity – white	0.02
Ethnicity – black	0.01

This is part of the modelling exercise: put variables in, run the segment solutions, see where BIC is best, look at significance and remove those that are insignificant, etc. While this seems time consuming, it ends up being far faster than, say, K-means, mostly because there is absolutely a good solution at the end, not an arbitrary quagmire of undifferentiated clusters.

The variables that end up being significant include:

Figure 10.3   Significant variables

Num DT purch
Num DT purch

Num electronics – TV purch
Num electronics – camera purch
Num electronics – printer purch
Num electronics – accessory purch
Num electronics – phone purch
Num electronics – sw – game purch
Num electronics – sw – productive purch

Num other – network purch
Num other – accessories purch
Num other – other purch

Number EM open
Number EM click

Number prod purch call centre
Number prod purch online

Number DM discount
Number EM discount

Num DM call
Num EM call
Num online config
Num online purch
Num call centre purch
Num call centre complaint

Q3 purchase
Q4 purchase
Avg time between purch (months)
Avg time between web visits (weeks)

Note that these variables are behavioural, as expected. Revenue variables are not even tested, as they are the RESULT of behaviour. Demographics typically are not significant and are also not behavioural. Of course, any and all of these variables can be used for profiling.

The next step is to correct for white noise, using bivariate residuals. This step adds a large number of parameters and will slow the analysis down. Way down. Analytically, all three dimensions are nudged simultaneously: find the number of segments, find the significant variables and correct with bivariate residuals.

The next step is to mark those bivariate residuals. These are indications of some pattern remaining that the independent variables are not eliminating. The bivariate residuals should be checked down to about 3.84. This is the 95% level of confidence (remember the 95% z-score for linear models is 1.96 and 3.84 = 1.96 * 1.96, a curvilinear metric).

The common last step is to run the second file through using the same number of segments, six, and the same variables found to be significant. Check the bivariate residuals and look at the two outputs. They should appear essentially the same. I usually do not statistically 'test' this sameness, I just look at it. I have never seen the two results to be different in any meaningful way.

Profile and output

The profile generally uses all the variables. Often there is a 'top-down' view and a 'bottom-up' view, or a strategy view and a tactical view, or a general view and a specific view. Below is the strategic, top-down or general view of the six segments (Table 10.5). This lens puts the segments together, to compare and contrast, all at once, looking at KPIs.

Table 10.5   General view of six segments

	Seg 1	Seg 2	Seg 3	Seg 4	Seg 5	Seg 6
% of market	30%	24%	19%	15%	9%	3%
% of revenue	32%	39%	9%	17%	2%	0%
# Total purch	14.49	25.64	8.88	18.17	7.95	9.65
Rev DT purch	3,150	4,730	999	2,592	352	81
Rev NB purch	2,320	720	680	1,152	630	168
Rev total purch	6,281	9,786	2,742	6,811	1,393	1,154
# DM sent	13.5	9.1	19.5	5.6	6.8	9.5
# EM sent	15.9	17.8	9.1	12.9	15.5	12.8
# EM open	1.4	3.2	0.4	4.5	1.7	2.6
# EM click	0.1	0.4	0	2.3	0.3	0.2
# Prod purch call centre	3.6	2.6	8	0.9	2	3.9
# Prod purch online	10.9	23.1	0.9	17.3	6	5.8
Education (years)	19.1	12.9	11.8	17.9	13.8	13.8
$ Income	185K	60K	45K	125K	15K	75K
% Q4 purchase	25%	70%	83%	14%	15%	41%
Avg time between purch	6.5	3.1	16.5	4.2	9.4	15.4
Avg time between web visits	3.2	2.1	9.5	1.9	3.9	8.5

A few quick comments can be made on the above output. First is that some demographics are shown. This is typical. Remember that while demographics are not statistically significant in designing the segmentation, they might still be of use in fleshing out the segments (and advertisers seem to love demographics). The first stage is partitioning and the second stage is probing. Adding additional data is part of the probing stage.

Let's look at the segmentation solution. Segment 1 is the largest in terms of market and each segment is successively smaller with segment 6 the smallest at 3%. The story is how segment size compares to per cent of revenue generated. Note that segment 2 contributes 39% of the revenue with only 24% of the market. Note that segment 5, conversely, is not pulling its fair share having 9% of the market but generating only 2% of the revenue. These metrics begin to let Scott know where he should put his resources and which segments are 'worth' marketing to. See the graph below (Figure 10.4).

Figure 10.4   % of market vs % of revenue

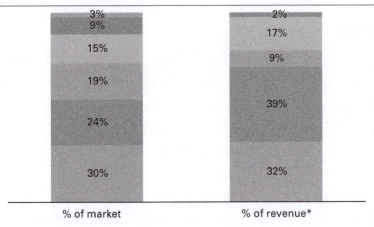

% of market   % of revenue*

* Does not add to 100% due to rounding.

Another story displays itself around channel preference. Segment 2 and segment 4 seem to be very web-centric, while segment 3 is NOT one that pursues online purchases. Segment 4 opens 4.5 of the 12.9 e-mails sent to them, whereas segment 3 opens 0.4 of the 9.1 e-mails sent to them. Segment 2 purchases 23.1 of their 25.64 products online (and segment 4 purchases 17.3 of their 18.17 products online) but again segment 3 purchases only 0.9 of their 8.88 products online. These are clear behavioural differences.

Segment 1 has the highest and segment 5 (mostly students, see below details) has the lowest income. Segment 1 has the most education and segment 2 the least education. The figures below show occupations and other demographics.

Comments/details on individual segments

A few notes and observations on each segment follow.

Segment 1

Segment 1 is the largest segment (30% of the market) and contributes 32% of the revenue.

Segment 1 purchases more desktops (3.5) and notebooks (2.9) than any other segment. They have a high penetration of productive software (twice the average) probably heavily invested in smart phone and tablet ownership, which means they are very high-tech comfortable.

Segment 1 receives the second-highest number of direct mails and e-mails sent. It's interesting to note, however, that they have the next-to-lowest number of e-mails clicked/number of e-mails open at 0.7%.

Segment 1 has the largest size household (4.1) and most (70%) white collar occupations. They have the highest income and highest education. They are youngish and probably could be called yuppies.

Segment 2

Segment 2 is the next-to-largest segment (24% of the market) and contributes more than their fair share of the revenue at 39%.

Segment 2 pays by far the highest desktop prices (75% above average) and has nearly four times higher than average gaming software purchases. Almost no productivity purchases, but a lot of accessory (nearly three times average) and phone purchases (nearly twice average).

Segment 2 shows next-to-highest number of e-mail opens and the highest number of products purchased online, 88% above average. This segment calls the call centre next-to-lowest number of times from the catalogue but has the highest number of calls from e-mails and they have the most online configurations.

This segment is the gamers! They tend to be young and single with next-to-smallest size of household. They purchase all of the gaming accessories: headphones, joystick, etc.

Segment 3

Segment 3 makes up 19% of the customer market but only accounts for 9% of the revenue. This segment does not come close to pulling its weight.

Segment 3 purchases a large amount of digital cameras (nearly twice average) and 50% more phones. When they do purchase they tend to buy low-end entry-level technology, which is one reason their revenue contribution is so low.

Segment 3 receives the highest number of catalogues and the lowest number of e-mails. This segment opens fewer and clicks less than any other. Segment 3 needs a (direct mail) discount in order to purchase.

Segment 3 calls from direct mail more and purchases from the call centre more than any other segment. Conversely, this segment calls from e-mail less and purchases online less than any other segment.

Segment 3 needs hand-holding. They are low tech and need a relationship to foster a purchase. They tend to be African-American, with a high percentage of blue collar and government occupations. This segment has the least education.

They call the call centre with complaints more than any other segment and tend to purchase mostly during the Christmas season.

Segment 4

Segment 4 is 15% of the market and generates 17% of the revenue.

Segment 4 purchases next-to-most desktops and next-to-most notebooks. They are very high tech, purchasing the most TVs, cameras, network and other accessories.

This segment has the highest e-mail opens and by far (over four times average) e-mail clicks than any other segment. They purchase fewer products from the call centre and next-to-most products purchased online than any other segment. They have the shortest time between web visits.

Segment 4 is very web-centric and probably believes 'print is dead!' They tend to be Asian, very high tech, with engineering white collar occupations. They would be early adopters, with next-to-highest education compared to other segments. They ignore direct mail and make most of their purchases online.

Segment 5

This segment is the least successful, being 9% of the market but only pulling 2% of the revenue.

Segment 5 purchases low-end products (few desktop, largely notebooks), mostly during back-to-school sales and usually with a discount. They purchase nearly zero consumer electronics.

Segment 5 receives the next-to-least number of direct mails and makes the next-to-least call centre purchases.

Segment 5 appears to be mostly students, single, unemployed, low income, etc.

Segment 6

Segment 6 is only 3% of the marketing and generates < 1% of the revenue.

Segment 6 really only purchases accessories and occasional items, spare parts, etc.

This segment is not really engaged in our brand, does not really respond to communications, etc. Segment 6 does not visit our website much and has the longest time between purchases. This segment might be a target to DE-market to. Note the high percentage of agricultural occupations.

Tables 10.6 and 10.7 present some details by segment, as referenced above.

Naming the segments

One of the most enjoyable exercises ever is the naming of the segments. A common way to do it is through revenue and products. This is the desktop segment and this is the low-tech segment, etc. Another possibility is with marcom. This is the direct mail responders and this is the e-mail preference segment, etc. Both of these are probably too simplistic.

Each segment name should have only two or three words to describe it: desktop devotees, gamers, life starters, web-centrics, etc. The idea is to be descriptive as well as memorable.

K-means compared to LCA

The comparison below came from Scott's debate with other analytic folks. Some of them had learned K-means and because LCA was new to them did not really understand or trust it. Therefore Scott ran LCA and told the K-means team the number of segments he found and he told them which variables to use. Note that these two pieces of information (how many segments and which variables to use are significant) would not ever be information K-means would have. Thus he gave the K-means team two HUGE advantages. Each team ran the algorithm and produced the KPIs in Table 10.8.

Notice in the top LCA table the variable 'Num total purch'. This table shows the averages by segment. Segment 2 on average purchases the most items, with 25.64 and segment 5 purchases the least items on average with 7.95. Look at the last column and see the high/low and 25.64/7.95 = 3.23. That is a measure of range, or dispersion.

See the lower part of the table which uses K-means. It is the same data, same number of segments and same variables used as significant. The high/low of Num total purch are much less different than that from LCA. A high of 17.7 and a low of 14.1 give a range of only 1.26. This is a typical difference. K-means output would work; LCA is simply better, more distinct and ultimately produces a clearer strategy.

Another fairly common finding comparing K-means to LCA is in terms of segment size. LCA produces segments ranging from 30% to 3%, but K-means ranges only from 24% to 9%. Because K-means produces roughly spherical clusters and they tend to be of similar size. There is no marketing theory that would hypothesize the segments should be of about the same size.

Scott convinced the team that the LCA output was the obvious way to go.

Elasticity modelling

One very natural and helpful exercise after segmentation is to do elasticity modelling. (Remember Chapter 4 on demand went through the modelling detail.) This shows different price sensitivities by segment. That is, one segment will likely be sensitive to price and another segment will likely NOT be sensitive to price, etc. This allows for very lucrative strategies. Review earlier chapters for how elasticity modelling is typically done.

Table 10.6 Details by segment

	Segment 1	Segment 2	Segment 3	Segment 4	Segment 5	Segment 6
% of market	30%	24%	19%	15%	9%	3%
% of revenue	32%	39%	9%	17%	2%	0%
Num DT purch	3.5	2.2	1.11	2.88	0.88	0.09
Num NB purch	2.9	1.2	0.85	1.44	1.05	0.21
Num electronics – TV purch	0.11	1.15	0.09	1.35	0.05	0.21
Num electronics – camera purch	0.02	0.05	1.06	1.88	0.24	0.45
Num electronics – printer purch	1.38	1.06	1.15	1.19	1.09	0.29
Num electronics – accessory purch	1.2	5.5	0.08	1.08	0.29	1.87
Num electronics – phone purch	0.03	1.21	0.99	0.89	0.09	0.35
Num electronics – sw – game purch	0.02	9.55	0.08	0.09	0.68	0.65
Num electronics – sw – productive purch	4.1	0.09	1.06	2.21	0.24	0.87
Num other – network purch	1.1	1.02	1.54	2.89	1.98	0.87
Num other – accessories purch	0.11	1.55	0.22	1.59	1.08	1.54
Num other – other purch	0.02	1.06	0.65	0.68	0.28	2.25

Num total purch	14.49	25.64	8.88	18.17	7.95	9.65
Rev DT purch	3,150	4,730	999	2,592	352	81
Rev NB purch	2,320	720	680	1,152	630	168
Rev electronics – TV purch	127	1,811	104	1,553	30	242
Rev electronics – camera purch	7	15	371	658	60	158
Rev electronics – printer purch	207	105	173	179	82	44
Rev electronics – accessory purch	90	853	6	81	19	140
Rev electronics – phone purch	7	454	223	200	14	79
Rev electronics – sw – game purch	1	716	5	6	37	42
Rev electronics – sw – productive purch	308	2	80	166	18	65
Rev other – network purch	61	97	85	159	109	48
Rev other – accessories purch	4	271	8	56	38	54
Rev other – other purch	0	12	10	10	4	34
Rev total purch	6,281	9,786	2,742	6,811	1,393	1,154

Table 10.7 Additional details by segment

	Segment 1	Segment 2	Segment 3	Segment 4	Segment 5	Segment 6
Number DM sent	13.5	9.1	19.5	5.6	6.8	9.5
Number EM sent	15.9	17.8	9.1	12.9	15.5	12.8
Number EM open	1.4	3.2	0.4	4.5	1.7	2.6
Number EM click	0.1	0.4	0	2.3	0.3	0.2
Number prod purch call centre	3.6	2.6	8	0.9	2	3.9
Number prod purch online	10.9	23.1	0.9	17.3	6	5.8
Number DM discount	8.1	5.5	11.7	3.4	4.1	5.7
Number EM discount	11.1	12.5	6.4	9	10.9	9
Number DM call	1.2	0.8	15.9	0.2	3.9	9.5
Number EM call	9.4	12.8	2.1	3.4	8.4	4.8
Num online config	5.5	21.5	0.7	16.5	12.6	0.4
Number call centre purch	3.6	2.6	8	0.9	2	3.9
Number call centre complaint	2.1	0.9	5.6	3.2	1.2	0.5

Age	28.9	25.5	41.9	30.1	21.2	38.9
Education (years)	19.1	12.9	11.8	17.9	13.8	13.8
Income	185,000	60,000	45,000	125,000	15,250	75,000
Size hh	4.1	1.2	3.9	3.7	1.1	3.1
Occupation – blue collar	20%	19%	60%	18%	13%	25%
Occupation – white collar	70%	38%	1%	65%	5%	35%
Occupation – agriculture	4%	5%	2%	1%	5%	18%
Occupation – government	3%	28%	25%	15%	15%	11%
Occupation – unemployed	1%	8%	10%	1%	60%	10%
Ethnicity – asian	15%	5%	2%	21%	7%	1%
Ethnicity – white	55%	65%	35%	41%	70%	80%
Ethnicity – black	20%	15%	35%	8%	10%	11%
Q1 purchase	30%	4%	6%	20%	5%	1%
Q2 purchase	25%	10%	5%	31%	5%	3%
Q3 purchase	20%	15%	5%	33%	75%	55%
Q4 purchase	25%	70%	83%	14%	15%	41%
Avg time between purch (months)	6.5	3.1	16.5	4.2	9.4	15.4
Avg time between web visits (weeks)	3.2	2.1	9.5	1.9	3.9	8.5

Table 10.8 KPIs

LCA output	Segment 1	Segment 2	Segment 3	Segment 4	Segment 5	Segment 6	hi/low
% of market	30%	24%	19%	15%	9%	3%	12
% of revenue	32%	39%	9%	17%	2%	0%	81.44
Num total purch	14.49	25.64	8.88	18.17	7.95	9.65	3.23
Rev DT purch	3,150	4,730	999	2,592	352	81	58.4
Rev NB purch	2,320	720	680	1,152	630	168	13.81
Rev total purch	6,281	9,786	2,742	6,811	1,393	1,154	8.48
Number DM sent	13.5	9.1	19.5	5.6	6.8	9.5	3.48
Number EM sent	15.9	17.8	9.1	12.9	15.5	12.8	1.96
Number EM open	1.4	3.2	0.4	4.5	1.7	2.6	12.4
Number EM click	0.1	0.4	0	2.3	0.3	0.2	124.04
Number prod purch call centre	3.6	2.6	8	0.9	2	3.9	8.8
Number prod purch online	10.9	23.1	0.9	17.3	6	5.8	25.99
Education (years)	19.1	12.9	11.8	17.9	13.8	13.8	1.62
Income	185,000	60,000	45,000	125,000	15,250	75,000	12.13
Q4 purchase	25%	70%	83%	14%	15%	41%	5.93
Time between purch (months)	6.5	3.1	16.5	4.2	9.4	15.4	5.32
Time between visits (weeks)	3.2	2.1	9.5	1.9	3.9	8.5	5

% of market	24%	19%	17%	16%	15%	9%	2.67
% of revenue	19%	15%	17%	19%	18%	13%	1.45
Num total purch	14.1	17.7	16.2	14.8	16.9	17.2	1.26
Rev DT purch	1,901	2,490	3,498	4,021	2,011	2,666	2.12
Rev NB purch	1,344	1,108	1,655	1,100	1,100	911	1.82
Rev total purch	4,992	5,006	6,271	7,509	7,489	9,200	1.84
Number DM sent	10.1	11	11.2	12.8	12.9	15.1	1.5
Number EM sent	11.9	15.2	16.4	15.2	14.9	15	1.38
Number EM open	1.8	2.2	2.3	2.2	2.1	2.8	1.56
Number EM click	0.61	0.66	0.54	0.52	0.51	0.26	2.54
Number prod purch call centre	3.1	3.6	3.7	3.9	3.4	4.9	1.58
Number prod purch online	9.1	10.2	12.4	17.1	13.5	13.6	1.88
Num total purch	12.2	13.8	16.1	21.0	16.9	18.5	1.73
Education (years)	16.3	16.4	15.1	13.1	15.3	15.5	1.25
Income	109,655	109,166	98,066	98,054	97,112	88,055	1.25
Q4 purchase	39%	34%	61%	44%	44%	55%	1.79
Time between purch (months)	6.6	7.5	7.7	9.1	8.1	7.9	1.38
Time between visits (weeks)	3.8	4.1	4.5	4.6	3.5	4.9	1.4

What Scott found was that segment 1 is not sensitive to price. This segment does not require a discount in order to purchase. He found conversely that segments 3 and 5 are very sensitive to price. These are the segments that will only buy with some kind of promotion.

Test and learn plan

The last step tends to be putting together some kind of testing plan. We will cover statistical details later in the book, but the concept is straightforward.

The idea is to corroborate the sensitivities the segmentation found. That is, if a segment is sensitive to price, test that. If a segment prefers a particular channel, test that, etc.

Usually selection is tested first, then promotion and then channel or product category, etc. These are usually in a test vs control situation.

WHY GO BEYOND RFM?

(This article was published in a different format in
Marketing Insights, April 2014)

Abstract

While RFM (recency, frequency and monetary) is used by many firms, it in fact has limited marketing usage. It is really only about engagement. It is valuable for a short-term, financial orientation but as organizations grow and become more complex a more sophisticated analytic technique is needed. RFM requires no marketing strategy and as firms increase in complexity there needs to be an increase in strategic planning. Segmentation is the right tool for both.

RFM has been a pillar of database marketing for 75 years. It can easily identify your 'best' customers. It works. So why go beyond RFM? To answer that, let's make sure we all know what we're talking about.

What is RFM?

One definition could be, 'An essential tool for identifying an organization's best customers is the recency/frequency/monetary formula.' RFM came about more than 75 years ago for use by direct marketers. It was especially popular when database marketing pioneers (such as Stan Rapp, Tom Collins, David Shepherd and Arthur Hughes) started writing their books and advocating database marketing (as the next generation of direct marketing) nearly 50 years ago. It became a popular way to make a database build (an expensive project) return a profit. Thus, the most pressing need was to satisfy finance.

Jackson and Wang wrote, 'In order to identify your best customers, you need to be able to look at customer data using recency, frequency and monetary analysis (RFM)...' (Jackson and Wang, 1997). Again the focus is on identifying your best customers. But, it is not marketing's job to just identify your 'best' customers. 'Best' is a continuum and should be based on far more than merely past financial metrics.

The usual way RFM is put into place, although there are an infinite number of permutations, ends up incorporating three scores. First, sort the database in terms of most recent transactions and score the top 20%, say, with a 5 and on down to the bottom 20% with a 1. Then re-sort the database based on frequency, maybe with the number of transactions in a year. Again, the top 20% get a 5 and the bottom 20% get a 1. The last step is to re-sort the database on, say, sales dollar volume. The top 20% get a 5 and the bottom 20% get a 1. Now, sum the three columns (R + F + M) and each customer will have a total ranging from 15 to 3. The highest scores are the 'best' customers.

Table 10.9 Customer totals

Customer ID	R	F	M	Total
999	3	2	1	6
1001	5	3	3	11
1003	4	4	2	10
1005	1	5	2	8
1007	1	4	1	6
1009	2	4	3	9
1010	3	4	4	11
1012	2	3	5	10
1014	3	1	5	9
1016	4	1	4	9
1017	5	2	3	10
1018	4	3	4	11
1020	4	4	3	11
1022	3	5	3	11
1024	2	4	2	8
1026	1	3	5	9

Note that this 'best' is entirely from the firm's point of view. The focus is not about customer behaviour, not about what the customer needs, why those with a high score are so involved or why those with a low score are not so engaged. The point is to make a (financial) return on the database, not to understand customer behaviour. That is, the motivation is financial and not marketing.

RFM works as a method of finding those most engaged. It works to a certain extent, and that extent is selection and targeting. RFM is simple and easy to use, easy to understand, easy to explain and easy to implement. It requires no analytic expertise. It doesn't really even require marketers, only a database and a programmer.

Say you re-score the database every month, in anticipation of sending out the new catalogue. That means that every month each customer potentially changes RFM value tiers. After every time period a new score is run and a new migration emerges. Note that you cannot learn why a customer changed their purchasing patterns, why they decreased their buying, why they made fewer purchases or why the time between purchases changed. Much like the tip of an iceberg, only the blatant results are seen and RFM gives nothing in the way of understanding the underlying motivations that caused the result- ant actions. There can be no rationale as to customer behaviour because the purpose of the algorithm used was not for understanding customer behav- iour. RFM uses the three financial metrics and does not use an algorithm that differentiates customer behaviour.

Because RFM cannot increase engagement (it only benefits from what- ever level of involvement, brand loyalty, satisfaction, etc you inherited at the time – with no idea WHY) it tends to make marketers passive. There is no relationship building because there is no customer understanding. That is, because RFM cannot provide a rationale as to what makes one value tier behave the way they do, marketing strategists cannot actively incentivize deeper engagement.

RFM is a good first step, but to make a great step requires something beyond RFM. Marketers require behavioural segmentation in order to prac- tise marketing.

What is behavioural segmentation?

Behavioural segmentation (BS) quickly followed RFM, due to the frustrations that RFM produced good, but not great, results. As with most things, complex analysis requires complex analytic tools and expertise. BS was put into place to apply marketing concepts when using a database for marketing purposes.

In order to institute a marketing strategy, there needs to be a process. Kotler recommended the four Ps of strategic marketing: partition, probe, prioritize and position. Partitioning is the process of segmentation.

While it's mathematically true that partitioning only requires a business rule (RFM is a business rule) to divide the market into sub-markets, behavioural segmentation is a specific analytic strategy. It uses customer behaviour to define the segments and it uses a statistical technique that maximally differentiates the segments. James H Myers even says, 'Many people believe that market segmentation is the key strategic concept in marketing today'.

BS is from the customer's point of view, using customer transactions and marcom response data to specifically understand what's important to customers. It is based on the marketing concept of customer-centricity. BS works for all strategic marketing activities: selection targeting, optimal price discounting, channel preference/customer journey, product penetration/category management, etc. BS allows a marketer to do more than mere targeting.

An important point might be made here. Behaviours are caused by motivations, both primary and experiential. Behaviours are purchases, visits, product usage and penetration, opens, clicks and marcom responses, etc. These behaviours cause financial results, revenue, growth, lifetime value and margin.

Primary motivations would be unseen things like attitudes, tastes and preferences, lifestyle, value set on price, channel preferences, benefits or need arousal. There are experiential, secondary causes of behaviour, typically based on some brand exposure. These are not behaviours, but cause subsequent behaviours. These secondary causes would be things like loyalty, engagement, satisfaction, courtesy or velocity. Note that RFM uses recency and frequency, metrics of engagement, which is a secondary cause. RFM also uses monetary metrics, which are resultant financial measures. Thus RFM does not use behavioural data, but engagement and financial data. These are very different than behavioural data used in BS. One simple way to distinguish behavioural data from secondary data is that behaviours are nouns: purchases, responses, etc. Note that secondary causes are adjectives: *engagement* metrics, *loyal* customers, *recent* transactions, *frequently* purchased, etc.

BS typically requires analytic expertise to implement. Behavioural segmentation is a statistical output (see Table 10.9).

One critical difference between BS and RFM is that in a behavioural segmentation members typically do not change groups. That is, the behaviour that defines a segment evolves very slowly. For example, if one person is sensitive to price, her defining behaviour will not really change. She is sensitive to price even after she has a baby, she is sensitive to price as she ages, or if she gets a puppy, or buys a new house. Her products purchased might change, her interests in certain campaigns might change, but her defining behaviour will not change. This is one of the advantages of BS over RFM. This is what drives your learning about the segments. BS provides such insights that each segment generates a rationale, a story, as to why it's unique enough to BE a segment.

While RFM uses only three dimensions, BS uses any and all behavioural dimensions that best differentiate the segments. It typically requires far more than three variables to optimally distinguish a market.

Because marketing mix testing can be done on each segment (using product, price, promotion and place) the insights generated make for differentiated marketing strategies for each segment. To test if RFM tiers drive behaviour is probably inappropriate, because tier membership potentially changes every time period. Much like studies that proclaim, 'women who smoke give birth to babies with low birth weight', there is spurious correlation going on. Just as another dimension (socio-economic, culture, etc) might be the real (unseen) cause of the low birth weight and NOT necessarily (only) the smoking, so there are other dimensions of (unseen) behaviour using RFM to explain, say, campaign responses. That is, the response is not caused by the RFM tier, but some other motivation.

In short, BS goes far beyond RFM. The insights and resultant strategies are typically worth it.

What does behavioural segmentation provide that RFM does not?

As mentioned, BS delivers a cohort of segment members that are maximally differentiated from other segment members. Because these members typically do not change segments, various marketing strategies can be levelled at each segment to maximize cross-sell, up-sell, ROI, margin, loyalty, satisfaction, etc.

BS identifies variables that optimally define each segment's unique sensitivities. For example, one segment might be defined by channel preference, another by price sensitivity, another by differing product penetrations and another by a preferred marcom vehicle. This knowledge, in and of itself, generates vast insights into segment motivations. These insights allow for a differentiated positioning of each segment based on each segment's key differentiators. You get away from trying to incentivize customers out of the 'bad' tiers and into the 'good' tiers. In BS, there are no good or bad tiers.

Your job is now to understand how to maximize each segment based on what drives that segment's behaviour, rather than focus on only migration. Thus, BS gives you a test-and-learn plan.

Because of the insights provided, knowledge is gained of each segment's prime pain points, which means that each segment can be treated with the right message, at the right time, with the right offer and at the right price. This kind of positioning creates a 'segment of one' in the customer's mind. This uniqueness differentiates the firm, perhaps even to the extent of moving it away from heavy competition and toward monopolistic competition. This means you approach a degree of market power that is becoming a price maker.

Because BS provides such insights it tends to make marketers very active in understanding motivations. This tends to generate very lucrative strategies for each segment.

Conclusion

What are the advantages of RFM? It's fast, simple and easy to use, explain and implement. What are the disadvantages of behavioural segmentation? It requires analytic expertise to generate, is more costly and takes longer to do.

BS takes behavioural variables and uses them for the purpose of understanding customer behaviour, and it uses a statistical algorithm to maximally differentiate each segment based on behaviour (see box below). As mentioned, the vast majority of marketers that evolve from RFM to BS say it's worth it, and their margins agree.

Segmentation techniques

There are three characteristics that distinguish behavioural segmentation from RFM: BS uses (typically) more behavioural data, BS uses the data for the specific purpose of understanding customer behaviour and BS uses statistical techniques to maximally separate the segments.

A short comparison from RFM to CHAID to K-means to latent class is instructive. RFM is multivariable (typically using three variables) but it is not multivariate – simultaneously using the three dimensions. RFM is mathematical and could not be a statistically valid option.

CHAID (chi-squared automatic interaction detection) is sometimes offered as a segmentation solution. It is a tree-like structure that splits the nodes based on the chi-square test. While CHAID is fast and simple (and probably better than RFM) it cannot be optimal. CHAID is not a statistical model but a heuristic, a guideline. It brings with it no diagnostics and little intelligence.

K-means (also called partition, iterative or clustering) is another fast and simple technique. The typical algorithm requires you to decide on the number of clusters (as if you know) and decide which variables to use to design the clusters (as if you know). K-means gives no diagnostics to aid in these important criteria, leaving it to your arbitrary intuition.

So, after the number of clusters is decided, along with which variables to use for clustering, the algorithm goes to the first observation (eg, customer on the dataset) that has all the variables populated, calculates the centroid (average of all the variables in dimensional space) and labels this cluster 1. It goes to the next observation that is populated, calculates the centroid and ascertains how far away (based on the square root Euclidean distance) the second observation is from the first. If it's 'far enough' away (based on criteria the analyst gives or a default) to be defined as its own cluster, it is. It continues through the dataset until the number of clusters supplied is created and all of the observations are classified into one (mutually exclusive) cluster.

Note: 1) It is not statistical, but mathematical. It uses the square root Euclidian distance to assign cluster membership. 2) Cluster centroids (and hence clusters) are highly dependent on the order of the dataset. If the dataset is re-sorted there will likely be very different segments. 3) It offers little in the way of diagnostics. 4) Because the clusters are naturally spherical (owing to assignments based on distance from a centroid) the clusters tend to be of similar size, which seems an unlikely assumption in a real market. While K-means is a step above RFM and CHAID, it clearly suffers from many shortcomings.

Latent class analysis (LCA) has been around for 50 years, but in the last 20 has really caught on. LCA is a Bayesian (maximum likelihood) technique, which is statistical in nature. Because customer behaviour is probabilistic (even irrational) a statistical technique better matches behaviour than a mathematical technique. It has diagnostics to find the optimal number of segments. It has diagnostics to find which variables are significant for the segmentation.

LCA applies a probability score to every observation (customer on the dataset) to belong to each segment. For example, it's one thing if customer

A is 95% likely to belong to segment 1 and only 5% likely to belong to segment 2. There is an obvious conclusion. But what if, owing to the customer as either newer on file or having displayed some unusual patterns, it is scored at 55% likely to belong to segment 1 and 45% likely to belong to segment 2? This is not so clear. LCA gives you the ability to remove from the segment assignments any of those that do not figure strong segment behaviour. This should typically be a very small percentage of the file but the ability to 'know' where each customer most likely belongs is very important strategically.

It has been proved often, but by none better than Jay Magidson and Jeroen K Vermunt, that LCA is vastly superior to K-means in terms of segment identification and separation (Magidson and Vermunt, 2002). Given the advantages of LCA as seen above, it should be seen as the first and best choice.

Checklist

You'll be the smartest person in the room if you:

☐ Remember SAS gives a metric of an optimal segmentation solution as the 'log of the determinant of the covariant matrix'.

☐ Recall a variety of segmentation techniques: business rules, CHAID, hierarchical clustering, K-means, latent class analysis (LCA), etc.

☐ Point out that LCA provides the optimal number of segments, diagnosis of which variables are significant and calculates a probability score for every member belonging to every segment – nothing is arbitrary!

☐ Use the behavioural segmentation process: strategize, collect behavioural data, create/use additional data, run the chosen algorithm and profile segment output.

☐ Prove RFM is from the firm's point of view and not the consumer's.

☐ Preach RFM incites no strategy except migration.

PART FOUR
More important topics for everyday marketing

Statistical testing 11

How do I know what works?

Everyone wants to test

Statistical testing (design of experiments, DOE) seems to decrease the risk of making a mistake.

> **Design of experiments:** an inductive way of creating a statistical test using a stimulus taking into account variance, confidence, etc, by randomization and comparison to a control group.

I'll tell you right now, I myself am not really a testing guy. I see its worth, but the times that the test is actually 'clean', can be measured and is measuring what it was designed to measure, are very few. This is because of a couple of things. First, companies do not want to design for test vs control – why would they want to take potential buyers out of the treatment (ie, the control group does not get the stimulus – the test)? The marketing science answer is that 'you must invest in the test!' So firms usually fight to make the control group so small, actually too small, so that a statistical (t-test, z-test, etc) cannot (reliably) be performed.

Another reason is that most of the time the test is 'dirty'. We never seem to get customers that were to get only a certain kind (or no kind) of treatment (stimulus). Say a customer is supposed to get treatment X so they can be measured against treatment Y (that is the test). However, accidentally, that customer also gets stimuli from other parts of the company and the number one rule of testing is: only one thing can be different in measuring test vs control. If a customer was supposed to get only treatment X and they (or some of them) also got stimulus A and treatment B, promotion C, etc, the test cannot be done; you cannot measure (in a DOE framework) multiple differences (without designing for that). That is why the design is critical.

Very few companies are disciplined enough to actually carry out a test. Most of the time, at the end of the test, everyone shrugs their shoulders and also acknowledges seasonality or competition or changing tastes and preferences or hypothesizes that something systematic affected the test results. So they want to test again. And again: never really learning in order to act, just testing. More about that later.

Sample size equation: use the lift measure

Testing questions always begin with sample size. The idea is to have a sample large enough – and with enough variation – in order to be confident about generalizing to the population. Remember statistics uses inductive reasoning. That is the point of testing: take a small sample (so as not to (publicly) ruin anything) and simulate the population. That's important. What you're trying to do is design a laboratory that looks (and acts) just like the population. You experiment on the (sampled) laboratory and find what seems to work and then you have to thrust these onto the population, which you hope will act as the sample did. That's inductive reasoning.

So we have to revisit the normal distribution, z-scores and the confidence interval. That was a long time ago, so go back if you need to. I did.

Remember that the normal distribution (although kind of theoretic) is the model that we use (mostly) for testing. We assume a normal distribution. The normal distribution is characterized by two things: 1) the mean and median and mode are all the same number and 2) their distribution is symmetrical about that number. Now, by definition, within the first standard deviation of a normal distribution are contained 68% of all the observations; with the second standard deviation add 14% to each side, aggregating 28% more for a total number of observations between two deviations of 96%. See Figure 11.1. Now let's think about z-scores. Remember the formula is

(observation – mean) / standard deviation.

Figure 11.1 Z-scores

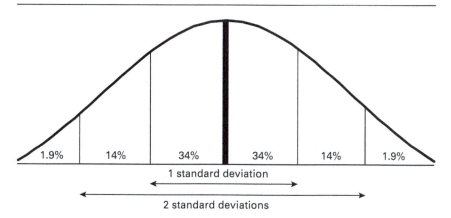

In terms of IQ, where the mean is 100 and the standard deviation is 15, 68% of all observations are between 85 and 115. Said another way, an IQ of +1 standard deviations is a z-score of 1.00, which is greater than (34 + 34 + 14 + 1.9) nearly 84% of the population. A z-score of +2.0 is greater than nearly 98% of the population. See? This is actually the key to sample size needed and overall testing.

By sample I mean a subset of the population. Even if you do not really have the whole, entire population, we'll pretend. What else can we do? So we generally take a simple random sample (SRS) of the population. But how large a sample do we need in order to simulate the population?

Sample size needs to take into account (in terms of DOE) variation which affects confidence. We are trying to be pretty confident that the size of our sample will mirror the population when the testing is done and then generalized to the population. That is, if you took the mean of the population and found it to be 50.0 and then took an SRS and found that mean to be 40.0, would you be confident that your sample mirrored the population? The answer is, 'Maybe, depending on the variation'. Say you knew the population had a mean of 50.0 but a standard deviation of 25.50. It's possible your SRS is representative of the population. The z-score is −0.392, which might not be THAT unusual.

So, the formula I'd advocate for sample size needs to take into account the standard deviation of the population, how confident you want to be of generalizing your results to the population after the test, what sensitivity you want to measure (ie, lift detection) and expected response. That is:

$$n = \frac{4Z^2(r)(1 - r)}{(rl)^2}$$

where n is sample size, Z is confidence level, r is response rate and l = lift detection. As an example, say we have an expected response rate of 28%, a confidence wanted of 90% (z-score = 1.64) and a minimal lift detection of 5%, the sample size needed in each cell is 5,566. That is, to be 90% confident your results will generalize to the population (9 out of 10 times it will, theoretically), and having usually a 28% response rate and you wanted to not detect a difference unless it is by at least 5% (that is, 26.6% – 29.4%) response, you need a total sample of 11,131. That is, for A/B testing you need 5,566 in each (test and control) cell. See?

I have to mention a silly thing that is still going on, I hear it all the time. The answer to the question 'How large a sample size do I need?' is often '380'. (If not exactly 380 it is very close to 380.) Let me show you where this comes from and why it is wrong. Even stupid.

The formula this uses is:

$$n = \left(\frac{z}{err}\right)^2 R(1 - R)$$

Often marketers test at 95% confidence (a z-score of 1.96) and a 1% response rate is assumed and they only want to accept a 1% error, which translates this formula into a sample size 380. Now think about this. A 1% assumed response rate means that of the 380 cell only 3.8 will respond. I guarantee that 3.8 (okay, round it up to 4 people) is NOT enough to be confident about. At all. Or if they say 380 are responses, then that cell actually had 38,000 in it, right? See the folly?

Isn't this the same problem with the formula I recommend above? No, it is not. Of the 5,566 cell size and a response rate of 28% that means there will be 1,558 responders and I can be confident with that. Or even at a 1% response rate (still 90% confidence and 5% lift) the cell size is over 200,000. And 2,000 responses are enough to test and be confident about. So, do not let them tell you 380 is an adequate sample size. Is it any wonder corporations are in a nose dive?

A/B testing and full factorial differences

A couple of quick notes on very common testing will follow. Did I mention I am not really a testing guy?

We always talk about A/B testing (sometimes called 'champion/challenger') and this simply means comparing (even as test vs control) two cells against each other. The idea is that we randomly chose the participants in each cell and (this is important) the only difference (get that? The only difference) between them is that the test cell has the test treatment and the control cell does not.

Then we measure the average responses of cell A vs cell B and if they are different enough we say they are statistically/significantly different. That means we have confidence (typically 95%) that when we generalize this to the population the same results happen, on a larger scale. The formula I usually use for response testing is the z-score:

$$Z = \frac{\dfrac{rA}{nA} - \dfrac{rB}{nB}}{\sqrt{p(1-p)\left(\dfrac{1}{nA} + \dfrac{1}{nB}\right)}}$$

where $p = \dfrac{rA + rB}{nA + nB}$. At 95% confidence if this formula is > 1.96 then the A response rate is statistically, significantly (and positively – yes this is very important!) different than the B response rate.

As an example, let's say for the A test we have responses of 1,200 and we sent 10,000. For B we have responses of 950 and we sent 5,000. rA means responses from A, nA means population of A. (rA = 1,200, nA = 10,000, rB = 950 and nB = 5,000.) This calculates to a z-score of –11.53 which is statistically and significantly different: with B out-performing A at 95% confidence.

Let me make another point that marketers (especially retailers) have a hard time with. In order to effectively calculate and monitor incremental marcom, there needs to be a universal control group (UCG). This means a group of customers that never (ever) get promoted to. This can be a small group, but still statistically significant in order to test. If you do not have a UCG you can only test one treatment compared to another, and never know if it's incremental (or detrimental for that matter). I realize I'm asking you to set aside a group of customers that will never get a promotion, never get a brand message, etc. This is called investing in the test. If knowledge (or proof) that your marcom is driving incremental revenue to your business is important (and no one would disagree that it is) then you need to invest in the test. Every campaign needs to be designed at least as a test vs control and the control is the UCG. If you do a business case on the potential revenue you'll lose from the UCG and compare that to the insight you'll have about which campaigns are actually increasing the bottom line, investing in a UCG wins every time. Remember the point of analytics is to decrease the chance of making a mistake and UCG is all about that.

BUSINESS CASE

Scott walked into the little conference room, knowing he would again have to explain similar concepts to last time with Becky, the director of consumer marketing, and the team. Every month she had many ideas about test-and-learn plans and what she wanted to learn from a series of mailings. Every month Scott had to re-clarify the concepts of testing, especially the idea of only changing one dimension at a time in order to test. He had thought if maybe he recorded last month's conversation he would just send the recording and replay it to everyone.

When they arrived, as expected Becky opened the conversation about testing their messages.

'I've thought about what you've been saying and have put a table together. We'd like to test discounts against different audiences.' She showed him the table. Note that discount level is applied only once. (See Table 11.1.)

Table 11.1 Testing discounts against different audiences

Cell A	5% discount	Desktop purchase
Cell B	10% discount	Online exclusive
Cell C	15% discount	Purchased >$2,500
Cell D	20% discount	Adding a printer

Scott sighed. 'This is the same idea we've had before. Compare two customers; one in cell A and another in cell B. If cell B has a higher response/more revenue, is it because of the 10% discounts or because of the online exclusive?'

'I would say both', Becky smiled.

'But the point of a test is to isolate just one treatment, in order to quantify that stimulus.' He looked at them. They all smiled, all nodded. 'What is needed to test this is not a 4 cell but a 16 cell matrix. Like this.' (He drew Table 11.2.)

'Wow', Becky said. 'That makes sense. We will need a far greater sample size though, right?'

'That's right. This is called full factorial and will detect all interactions. The benefit is in the confidence of the learnings and the cost is in the sample size, which means both time and money. It's a trade-off, as always.'

'Okay, we'll redesign. Let's also talk about the results of last month's test.'

'Great.'

Table 11.2 Testing discounts against different audiences in a 16 cell matrix

	5% discount	10% discount	15% discount	20% discount
Desktop purchase	Cell A	Cell E	Cell I	Cell M
Online exclusive	Cell B	Cell F	Cell J	Cell N
Purchased > $2,500	Cell C	Cell G	Cell K	Cell O
Adding a printer	Cell D	Cell H	Cell L	Cell P

'Well, in this case the control cell out-performed the test cell. So the test did not work.'

'What were we testing?'

'This was to past desktop purchasers. The control was a 10% discount and the test was a 20% discount. In the past the 10% discount is pretty standard so we wanted to see how many more sales happen with a 20% discount.'

'Makes sense', Scott said. 'It seems so weird that the 10% would out-perform the 20%. By how much?'

'By almost 50% more response, that is, number of purchases.'

'These were randomly chosen?'

'Yes', Becky said. 'I guess it means our target audience does not need a deeper discount, which is a good thing. They are very loyal and will act without a deeper stimulus. But somehow I doubt it.'

'So do I. It does not make economic sense. We should investigate the list, make sure both sides got the single treatment, try to see if something was amiss. Each cell was about the same size?'

'Yeah, very close.'

'But', Kristina said, 'how did we make sure both cells only got this treatment?'

'What do you mean?' Scott asked.

'Nothing happened that I know of to pull these customers out and only get this month's deal.'

'And last month the "Get a Free Printer" went out.'

'And the desktop bundle went out.'

'And since far more of our customers get the 10% discount than anything else, those that got the 10% discount in this test cell may also have received one or both of the other stimuli. Right?'

'Yeah, I think so.'

'Well, if true, that could explain it', Scott said. 'Our 10% test cell may have got at least three stimuli, not one.'

Becky sighed. 'So the test has to be done again?'

'Probably. If it was important to know what that treatment drove then the answer is yes.'

'Well, yeah it was. And we've had such difficulty with testing anyway – I mean the design of it – to go back and re-test will be a hard sell.'

Scott looked at her. 'I don't know how helpful it might be, but we possibly could do a multivariate exercise to try to isolate this test.'

'What do you mean?'

'I'm not sure. We might be able to do a model that accounts for all the treatments and still, *ceteris paribus*, measures just this campaign.'

Kristina looked up. 'You mean an ANOVA of some kind?' (Analysis of variance is a general statistical technique to analyse the differences within and between group means.)

'Yeah, although I'm an econ guy so I'm more comfortable with regression. But some technique that accounts for multiple simultaneous sources of stimuli on revenue.'

Scott went to the white board and drew Table 11.3.

Table 11.3   Multiple sources model

Cust ID	60 day review	Printer promo	DT bundle promo	20% disc promo	# opens	# clicks	# web visits	# calls	Past rev
X	0	1	0	1	7	3	9	0	1800
Y	900	0	1	1	8	1	5	2	490
Z	0	0	0	0	11	4	4	1	800

'Now', Scott said, 'we can include any and all promotions, etc, that we can track and put in this model. The idea is to measure the dollar value of all stimuli.'

'What if we don't or can't get all the information?'

'We will always miss something. It's important to include all we know, all we can know, from both a theoretical as well as actual causality assumption. There is a fine line between including too much and missing something important.'

'Can you explain a bit about that? I'm not sure what you mean', Kristina asked.

'From an econometric point of view, to exclude a relevant variable will bias those parameter estimates, so we need to ensure we have all important theoretically sound independent variables. To include an irrelevant variable increases the standard error of the parameters estimates, meaning that while they are unbiased the variation is larger than it should be so the t-ratios (beta/standard error of beta) will appear smaller than they should be. Thus, it behooves modellers to design a theoretically sound model and collect relevant data.'

They all looked at him. 'Sounds good', Becky said. 'Let's talk with IT and collect the data you need and you can put this together for us?'

So Scott got the data together and ran the model and they found the various campaigns' contribution to revenue that accounted for most other important factors. This type of analysis allowed Scott's team to offer campaign valuation outside of a strictly testing environment. While each point of view has pluses and minuses, Scott's valuation method could specifically take into account other (dirty) data issues. Also, his results directly tied to sales, something A/B testing did not do. As mentioned, a background in economics is valuable for a marketing science function.

Checklist

You'll be the smartest person in the room if you:

☐ Remind everyone that they must 'Invest in the test!' This typically means using a large enough sample for a control group that will allow a meaningful test.

☐ Point out that it's difficult to actually control for everything. Simple random selection is only a blunt instrument.

☐ Remember that experiment design, A/B testing (champion vs challenger) will not give the impact of individual dimensions (what impact price has, or message, or competition changes, etc).

☐ Demand that the sample size equation incorporates lift.

☐ Make fun of the silly answer ('N = 380') to the question 'How large a sample do we need?'

☐ Shout loud that in all testing each cell can only differ by one thing (one dimension).

☐ Recommend using ordinary regression to account for 'dirty' testing.

Implementing Big Data and Big Data analytics   12

Introduction

Okay, this has to be done. It's time. Earlier I hinted at it, now I'll address it. I've avoided it because Big Data (yes, you have to capitalize it) is everywhere. You can't get away from it. It's seemingly in every post, every update, every blog, every article, every book, every resume and every college class anywhere you look. It's inescapable. So now it's time to add to the fray.

What is Big Data?

No one knows. I'll provide a working definition here in 2018 but it will evolve over the years.

Big Data is BIG

By 'Big' I mean many, many rows and many, many columns. Note that there is no magic threshold that suddenly puts us in the 'Oh my, we are now in the Big Data range!' It's relative. This brings us to the second and third dimension of what is Big Data: complexity.

Big Data is multiple sources merged together

The dimensions of Big Data came about because of the proliferation of multiple sources of data, both traditional and non-traditional.

Traditional data means transactions from, say, a POS (point-of-sale system) and marcom (marketing communications) responses. This is what we've had for decades. We also created our own data, things like time between purchases, discount rate, seasonality, click-through rate, etc.

The next step was to add overlay data and marketing research data. This was third-party demographics and lifestyle data merged to the customer file. Marketing research responses could be merged to the customer file to provide things like satisfaction, awareness, competitive density, etc.

Then came the first wave of different data: web logs or clickstream data. This was different and the first taste of Big Data. It is another channel. Merging it with customer data is a whole other process.

Now there is non-traditional data. I'm talking about the merge-to-customer view. In terms of social media the merge-to-individual-customers is a whole technology or platform issue. But there are several companies who've developed technologies to scrape off the customer's ID: e-mail, link, handle, tag, etc and merge with other data sources. This is clearly a very different kind of data but it shows us, say, number of friends or connections, blog or post activity, sentiment, touch points, site visits, etc.

Big Data is multiple structures merged together

Big Data has an element of different degrees of structure. I'm talking about the very common structured data through semi-structured and all the way to unstructured data. Structured data includes the traditional codes that are expected by type and length – it is uniform. Unstructured data is everything but that. It can include text mining from, say, call records and free-form comments; it can also include video and audio and graphics, etc. Big Data allows us to structure this unstructured data.

Big Data is analytically and strategically valuable

Just to be obvious: data that is not valuable can barely be called data. It can be called clutter or noise. But it's true that what is clutter to me might be gold to you. Take clickstream data. That URL has a lot in it. To the marketing analyst, what is typically of value is the page the visitor came from and is going to, how long they were there, what they clicked on, etc. What web browser they used or whether it's an active server page or the time to load the wire frame (all probably critically important to some data scientist somewhere) is of little to no value to the marketer. So Big Data can generate a lot of stuff but there has to be a, say, text mining technique/technology to put it in a form that can be consumed. That's what makes it valuable –not the quantity but the quality.

Is Big Data important?

Probably. As alluded to above, multiple data sources can provide the marketer with insights into consumer behaviour. It's important in providing more touch points of the shopping and purchasing process. To realize that one segment always looks at word-of-mouth opinions and blogs for the product in question is very important. Recognizing that another segment reads reviews and puts a lot of attention on negative sentiment can be invaluable for marketing strategy (and PR!).

Just like 20 years ago, clickstream data provided another view of shopping and purchasing, Big Data adds layers of complexity. Because consumer behaviour is complex, added granularity is a benefit. But beware of 'majoring on the minors' or 'paralysis of analysis'. Aim at action!

What does it mean for analytics?
For strategy?

There needs to be a theory: THIS causes THAT. An insight has to be new and provide an explanation of causality and must be of a type that can be acted upon. Otherwise (no matter how BIG it is) it is meaningless. So the only value of Big Data is that it gives us a glimpse into the consumer's mindset: it shows us their 'path to purchase'.

For analytics this means a realm of attribution modelling that places weight on each touch point, by behavioural segment. Strategically, from a portfolio point of view, it tells us that *this* touch point is of value to shoppers/purchasers and *this* one is NOT. Therefore, attention needs to be paid to those (pages, sites, networks, groups, communities, stores, blogs, influencers, etc) touch points that are important to consumers. The biggest difference that Big Data offers is that now we have more things to look at – more complexity – and this cannot be ignored. To pretend consumers do not travel down that path is to be foolishly simplistic. For example, when a three-dimensional globe is forced into two-dimensional (from a sphere to a wall) space, Greenland looks to be the size of Africa. The over-simplification creates distortion. The same is true of consumer behaviour. The tip of the iceberg that we see is motivated by many unseen, below the surface, causes.

So what?

Big Data is not going to go away. And we will be better for it. Big Data is more about technology than analytic methods. While Big Data has been around for decades, only now, because of hardware or software advances and distributed processing (Hadoop), is analysis a reality. The new data does not require new analytic techniques. It may tap into and use more exotic algorithms. The new data does not require new marketing strategies. Marketing is still marketing and understanding and incentivizing and changing consumer behaviour is still what marketers do.

Surviving the Big Data panic

How many times have you heard the following:

- 'New data – different data – Big Data!'
- 'Quick, all hands on deck, we have a different data source.'
- 'Throw out all we know about analytics and consumer behaviour and marketing strategy and start from scratch.'
- 'There are new data sources! Obviously, the old ways need be eliminated and we desperately need to design new algorithms and new strategies.'

Sound familiar? How many meetings have you attended where everyone shook their heads in fear and panic? No one knows how to deal with these new sources of (unstructured) data. Divert all attention, stop everything now, because there are additional sources of consumer behaviour.

Okay, take a deep breath. I'll make a few confessions and the first one is that I've been around nearly (gulp!) thirty years doing marketing analytics.

There have always been waves of (new) data and they will continue. The 1970s introduced relational databases, storing data in hierarchical formats. Then in the 1980s came the emergence of business intelligence. That's when I started, doing analytics when we first merged POS with marcom responses. This is small data. We thought RFM was so analytic! I saw the first panic then. People reached for things like the Taguchi method, which was about measuring inanimate objects from the manufacturing industry! It was misguided and inappropriate but it looked and sounded very hip. New data sources required a new approach. Then we tested it in the field and it provided nothing but confusion.

The 1990s saw the introduction of the world wide web and the internet. Medium data! Clickstream data arrives, a new source of consumer behaviour. Of course, we thought we needed a new algorithm and new strategies. Somehow, we forgot it is still marketing, it is still consumer behaviour. Neural networks became vogue, at least until *Jurassic Park* came out and Jeff Goldblum uttered those mesmerizing words... chaos theory! For the next 10 years I heard all about unsupervised techniques and voodoo or black-box things geared more for mystics rather than insights. Enter SAS with Enterprise Minor! Fortunately, David Shepherd (of the Direct Marketing Association) offered a bounty on his website for any proof that unsupervised techniques out-performed traditional econometrics in the field. No one ever took that bounty.

This is not to say that digital data IS NOT very different from traditional data. I LOVE clickstream data that shows just what page a consumer views, for how long and in what order. That is an amazing tracking of consumer behaviour. And the new social media is bringing about a paradigm shift from outbound marketing to inbound marketing. The same can be said for telematics or sensor data, text, time and location data, RFID, etc. They're different kinds of data but why would they require new statistical techniques? Are they not still about quantifying causality?

Consumers are still behaving, shopping, choosing and buying. Right? I advocate a practical application of traditional techniques applied to different kinds of (non-traditional and otherwise) data.

I'm not against new algorithms when needed. Typically, I do not think they are needed. Below, I briefly list a few popular 'exotic' algorithms. I am philosophically opposed to many of the conceptions that seem to be behind these new techniques, in that they almost remove the analyst from the analysis. They make it automatic. Maybe I'm old-fashioned and just wrong-headed. The global chief strategy officer of a large prominent agency told me that the things I knew and the things I believed in are no longer valid. (He has a new job now, with a much, much smaller agency.)

Look: additional, different data does at least one good thing. It gives us new and deeper insights into consumer behaviour. For marketing analysts that is always a good idea. Additional complexity, as appropriate, is the right dimension to pursue. Over-simplification is wrong. Thus, added dimensions of complexity are valuable.

We do not need to search for exotic algorithms or knee-jerk into wildly different strategies. We need to embrace the layers of information we have about consumer behaviour and take all that into account. We have analytic techniques (and have had for decades) for doing that very thing: simultaneous equations, structural equations, vector auto regression, etc. Yes, these are more complex and that is where our attention should be: learning to perfect modelling that incorporates explaining additional complexity in consumer behaviour. After all, marketing is, and has always been about, understanding and incentivizing and changing consumer behaviour. That will be no different when the next wave of data hits.

Big Data analytics

One point I'd like to clear up: Big Data and analytics. It's easy to get lost in the techno-jargon around Big Data. In my simplistic view, let's say an analysis has these phases:

1 define the problem;
2 collect data;
3 apply algorithm;
4 implement/output solution.

In terms of Big Data, has that changed the first phase? No, probably not. The problem is still the same. Let's say marketers are trying to send communications to customers and get them to buy. Phase 1 is the same whether Big Data is included or used or accessible or not.

Phase 2 does require some of the Big Data tools and processes and techniques (map reduce, Hadoop, etc). Even some of the text mining will require the ability to turn unstructured data into structured data, so some natural language programming is necessary.

Now for our purposes, does Big Data require different algorithms? As mentioned above, my view is that (so far) it DOES NOT. Ordinary regression will work, logistic regression will answer many questions, segmentation is the right approach, etc. For Phase 4 I would suggest there are some Big Data tools to implement in real time.

So, in my contrived example of an analytics solution to a business problem, the framing of the questions and the analytics itself can be done independently of Big Data technology and processes. I'm trying to draw a line here that says the technology is on one side and the questions and analysis are on the other side. Disagree if you like.

With that said, I would like to go over the more common, promising new or 'exotic' algorithms, and try to place them in the marketing analyst's tool belt.

Big Data – exotic algorithms

The following section is designed as a brief and simple overview of a few key and popular techniques dealing especially with non-traditional data. No attempt is made to explain in detail how these work as there are hundreds of textbooks devoted to each of these. The idea is to give a sampling so curiosity can drive further investigation.

Earlier, this book classified broad statistical techniques into dependent equation types (ordinary regression, logistic regression, survival modelling, etc) and inter-relationship types (segmentation, factoring, etc).

The language of the algorithms below widen that definition into supervised, unsupervised and reinforcement learning:

- *Supervised learning* has a guiding (target) variable and is trying to predict that variable. These techniques include regression and classification types: decision trees, random forests, K-nearest neighbour, logistic regression, etc.

- *Unsupervised learning* does not have a guiding variable. These include segmentation and dimension reduction types: clustering, neural networks, factoring, etc.

- *Reinforcement learning* is where artificial intelligence (AI) lives and is about applying feedback loops into the algorithm. These are generally Markov-like processing (Q-learning, etc).

The overall story of 'exotic' algorithms (compared to the previously discussed 'traditional' algorithms) will tend to be: more dimensions of data provide more dimensions of insights and MAY require differently sophisticated techniques. These techniques may be more non-linear, more dimensional and less correlational. Now, a few words about three rising-in-popularity analytic techniques of which to be aware.

Neural networks

From a technique point of view, much of what has been covered so far has been regression or classification of a linear nature. That is, βXi. Most of what has gone before has involved only blatant variables. That is, a variable stands for what it measures. There is a family of non-linear, latent variable hypothesized, techniques called neural networks (NNs). NNs can be used for dependent variable techniques as well as inter-relationship techniques (classification).

An NN analyses input data through layers of 'neurons'. It looks for patterns in the input data. If a pattern is found, the next layer is activated. An association connection is built. This continues until convergence and the NN is ready to make a prediction.

A very common approach to NN technology is 'input variables, hidden variables and output variables connected by nodes' (see Figure 12.1). Every node is fully connected to all input and output variables. So there are three layers: the outputs of the input variables feed into the hidden variables; the outputs of the hidden variables feed into the output variables as inputs.

Figure 12.1   Example of a neural network

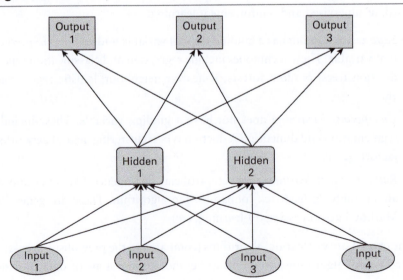

In a conceptual way, each layer is a system of models. The NN technique trains one layer to predict the next layer, etc. This gives rise to potentially complex, very well-fitting (sometimes over-fitting) models.

The down side is that an NN can be computationally expensive and can suffer from over-fitting. This is why training a dataset is so critical. NNs can create other variables, typically interactions, and these can be difficult to interpret. An NN has its place (computer vision, autonomous driving, AI implantations, etc) but from the marketing analyst's standpoint it does not aid in understanding the system being modelled. It can achieve accuracy but gives little inference.

Support vector machines (SVM)

Support vector machines, from decision sciences, are discriminant classifiers. That is, their purpose is to optimally separate data into groups.

Conceptually (see Figure 12.2) let's consider an example in two dimensions. Say there are training data points closest to the boundary. These data points are support vectors. The idea is to find the optimal line, given these support vectors. This line is optimal in that the distance (margin) from it to the nearest data points (support vectors) is maximized. This is done via Lagrange multipliers.

Figure 12.2   Example of a support vector machine

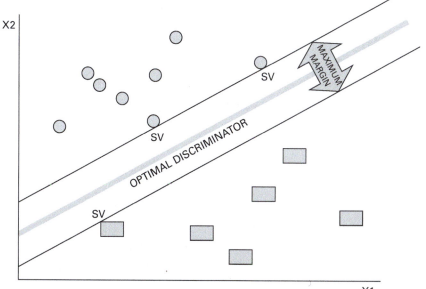

The dual (quadratic) optimization problem is: 1) to maximize under positivity constraints; and 2) an equality constraint. The maximization is finding the optimal separating line and the equality constraint is about having none of the training points (support vectors should be inside the margin).

Random forests

Random forests are part of ensemble models. (These became famous with Netflix's competition to build the best recommendation engine. The winning model was an ensemble technique.) Random forests combine several techniques into one super-model including segmentation, regression, etc. The output selects the consensus prediction of all the models.

Generally, random forests are about growing many (classification) trees. (That's why it's called a forest.) CHAID-like, a tree is grown by randomly sampling the cases and using the input variables to best split (explain) the variable (creating a node) above it. This is repeated selecting different input variables and finally aggregating all the outputs together. Note that decision trees are not the only input into general ensemble models.

Conceptually, why would an ensemble method be worthwhile? Because it has a chance to reduce error. In the language of control theory, say there are two sources of error: common cause and special cause. One or more modelling techniques may address common cause better (inherent bias, variance, etc) and another technique may account better for special cause (randomness, outliers, influential observations, etc).

Conclusion

Generally speaking, new data sources do not require new analytic techniques. I've given a brief overview of a few of the more popular techniques gaining support due to Big Data.

Checklist

You'll be the smartest person in the room if you:

☐   Do NOT panic.

☐   Keep a tight definition of WHAT Big Data is:

  – multiple data sources and multiple data types (potentially including video, audio, free-form text, etc).

☐   Remember that new data sources do NOT necessarily require new algorithms.

☐   Appreciate the advantages of complexity and additional insights into consumer behaviour, that is, think like a marketer and not a database analyst.

☐   Demand that traditional econometric techniques will still solve most marketing analytic questions.

☐   Realize that several new algorithms have increased in popularity:

  – neural networks, SVM and random forests.

PART FIVE
Conclusion

The finale 13

What should you take away from this?

What things have I learned that I'd like to pass on to you?

Wow, we're here at the end. I hope it was worthwhile and maybe a little fun. If so, tell your friends.

One thing I'd like the rest of the corporate world to know is what a marketing analyst does. That is, not the technical details but what is their function, what is their purpose, why are they important?

Now, I know that if we take a random sample of people all across a number of corporations and ask them, 'What are the first two words that come to mind, when you think of marketing analysts?'

Most of them will answer, 'Smouldering sexuality'.

I know it's true, we deal with real data, we see campaign effectiveness, we can forecast, it is no doubt the sexiest thing in the building. But that is not what I would want them to think about us, top of mind. I would hope that this book – and many like it – will help them to think of us as 'QUANTIFYING CAUSALITY'.

We are able to think in terms of 'this causes that', this variable (price) changes that variable (sales) and then – most importantly – quantify it so marketing strategy can act on it. We quantify causality.

I don't want to hear, 'Correlation is not causality' because who cares; we are not talking about correlation, and we hardly ever talk about correlation. Granger causality (invented by economist Clive Granger) asserts that if an X variable comes before the Y variable, and if the Y variable does not come before the X variable, and if, in removing the X variable, the accuracy of the prediction deteriorates, then therefore X causes Y. And we can state it as causality.

So, a couple of things I've learned that I'd like to pass on to you. These are anecdotes that helped me focus on important things and I hope these stories will help you.

Anecdote #1

My first job was as a salesman in a shoe store. I was 16 and that at least meant I thought everyone over 30 was out of touch and un-cool (it was the mid-1970s).

One day the boss was out and left Ben and I in charge of the store. Ben was a part-time sales guy, had known the boss and his family for years, was semi-retired and over 60 years old.

A woman came in dragging two toddlers with her. Ben was at the counter and the woman set down a pair of shoes and said the strap broke. Ben said he'd help her get a replacement. I saw right away those were NOT our shoes. That woman was about to get a free pair of shoes because of a slightly confused salesman. I was not able to get his attention to explain the error to him. He got her another pair of shoes and she also bought a pair for one of her toddlers. I watched them as she paid and checked out and Ben waved at her and smiled.

I went up to him. 'Ben, what are you doing?! Those were not our shoes!'

'Oh, you mean for Mrs. Rasmun?'

'Yes, you gave her a pair of shoes, for free!'

'Yes, I know her. She's a returning customer, has about five kids, comes in here all the time.'

'But, you GAVE her a pair of shoes.'

He looked at me. 'Yes. If I told her those were not our shoes she would have disagreed and walked out, unhappy, maybe not to ever come back. Maybe not buy her kids their shoes here. I did give her a pair of shoes. I also sold her another pair of shoes, and ensured she was satisfied and would continue to come back.'

I gulped. 'Oh...'. So much for my coolness.

What I took away from that, other than my narrow-minded profiling, was that smartness is always about focusing on the customer. It's not what is 'right' financially, but what drives a business is customer-centricity. That's probably why I ended up in marketing, a discipline that (is supposed to) put customers first.

Now, does this mean the customer is always right? Of course not, see above. The customer CAN be crazy. Remember Gary Becker's irrational demand curve (Becker, 1962). But, according to Peter Drucker, the purpose of a business is to create and keep a customer – get it? KEEP a customer. This means understanding a customer, and this means using analytics.

What to get out of this: being customer-centric is always right.

Anecdote #2

I worked early on as an analyst at a PC manufacturing firm. I was also finishing my PhD; in fact, writing my dissertation. It involved a fairly novel kind of mathematics, called tensor analysis (more used in physics/engineering than marketing/economics) and was about modelling multi-dimensional demand. My boss (while not very analytic, was very strategic – including promoting his group and himself to all of his bosses) was impressed with the idea.

Somehow he got an appointment with the CEO, three levels above himself, to show my dissertation. This was not about the differential geometry of manifold tensors, but what could be done for the PC manufacturing company in terms of better estimates of demand. So the big meeting was set, about five weeks in advance to give us time to prepare – no pressure! This was an important meeting with the CEO – no pressure! So we (my boss, call him Bob, and I) worked hard on the PowerPoint presentation, spending days on the words and graphics, trying to focus on the use cases of demand for PCs. HR and the CEO's secretary even made us practise our delivery in front of them. Finally it was all done and we had our time with the CEO.

We went in and the office was like a museum, glass and brass and marble – it was a corporate temple.

'So', my manager, Bob, began, 'thanks so much for some of your time. Mike here has a very interesting PC model to show you. Mike?'

I cleared my throat and pointed to the overhead projection. 'Demand is usually modelled as units being a function of several things, including price. It is always about holding everything else constant.'

'So Bob', the CEO said, 'how are we going to beat the competition on these server wars?'

I looked at him. What?

'Oh', Bob stammered, 'we have some ideas in mind.'

The next 45 minutes was about Bob and the CEO talking about the server wars and our competition. At the end we shook hands and left.

What to get out of this: success comes from focusing on what's impor-
tant, especially on what's important to those several levels above you.

Anecdotes #3 and #4

This anecdote is important, because anyone doing marketing science has faced it. And those not in marketing science wonder about it. I'm talking about altering the data, editing the output file, changing the results to be (more) intuitive.

This is the underbelly of marketing science. I know those in other functions wonder if we change the data. Do we make stuff up?

A client recently told me about a consultant who was predicting the lift they would get on a particular campaign. The consultant estimated a 16% increase, which was significantly MORE than anything ever achieved before. The consultant was unsure on what were the key drivers of this phenomenal success. The client frankly did not believe it and said so. The consultant asked what it should be and the client replied that about one-tenth of his estimate would be believable. The next week the consultant came back with a revised estimate of, wait for it, 2%. One-tenth of what their analytics had predicted earlier. Now I'm here to tell you that there is no way a model would predict 16% and then revise it to realistically be 2%, assuming real analytics were done.

That is one of the only instances I know of where they simply changed the output file. By the way, the client did not believe it either (did not trust their analytics) and fired them. Rightfully so.

So, do we change the output file? The answer is no. We can't. It's not just about intellectual integrity, it's about COA (covering our asses!). Altering the data cannot be hidden; changing the results cannot be buried deep enough to never be found. That is, you will be found out, you will be caught and they will know that you altered the results. You will never have credibility again. It cannot be hidden. Trust me, it will (eventually) be discovered. This is because all data is interrelated, one metric drives another, and one piece affects another because one variable fits together with another to tell the whole story. Changing one part of it will affect all other parts and it will NOT add up. That does not mean you have to broadcast it to everyone though. You can emphasize this or direct the conversation to focus on that.

The biggest mistake I've ever made (that I know of) was ridiculously simple but very costly. I was a database marketing analyst and my job was to do a model and produce a list for customers most likely to purchase. We sent out over a million catalogues a month (at a cost of about 0.40 each).

I developed a logistic regression model to score the database with probability to buy and used SAS proc rank. I was supposed to give them the top three deciles. Now, SAS proc rank has decile output labelled from 0 to 9, with 0 the highest (the best). I accidentally sent deciles 7, 8 and 9 – the lowest, the worst. Although these were the highest (numbered) deciles, get it? Easy mistake to make, right? Well, the campaign that month did not do well. So I sent a message to everyone that I was working on a new model that I thought might be better for next month. My message was designed as a preemptive strike that I was engaged and working on the problem. That's what they saw, I was making it better. When the time arrived the following month I used the same model but this time picked deciles 0, 1 and 2 (the best). That campaign worked well. I was congratulated on improving the model. Of course my team knew it was the same model but the right deciles were chosen. Key takeaway: be careful and be upfront and honest (as need be).

Another anecdote from early in my career was about demand estimation. My job was to forecast call volume and based on that volume different load-balancing (among other things) sites were designed. Well, the company had decided to build another site (in Florida) to handle all the calls. They had bought the land and got a building and were hiring people to staff it. Eventually someone thought maybe they should predict how many calls would go there, that is, estimate demand. It so happened that my boss was a well-respected and long-time econometrician and our job was to put up the demand numbers. Everyone knew the demand was huge; the question was just how huge. So I collected data, macro and micro variables, competition, new products, time series trends, etc. The forecast I got was low – way lower than expected. I gulped and looked at it again. The model was forecasting less than half what was needed for a new site. I met with my boss and we went over everything but could only assume, in the best scenario, 60% of what was needed. We gave the real estate team our estimates and they said thanks and then carried on with the building and the hiring for the new site. A year later that site was closed – there was not enough call volume to support it.

Now it would have been easy and acceptable for us to just double the output, right? It would have been easy to make heroic assumptions that made no sense in order to get the demand forecast way higher, right? In this case we just showed the output and shrugged our shoulders and called it a conservative, worst case scenario.

To have altered it would have been akin to what Einstein called the biggest blunder of his life (not that I'm comparing myself to him!). Einstein's relativity equations showed that because of gravity the universe should be expanding (or contracting). Since no one believed that, including

Einstein himself, he added a 'cosmological constant' to his equations, in effect a mathematical way to cancel out the expansion. A few years later Hubble discovered that the universe was indeed expanding. Einstein edited the output file! The key takeaway? If it did not work for Einstein it will not work for you. Do not change the results.

What other things should you take away from all this?

Have an implementation plan!

The best analytics in the world is of no use if it is not implemented. Often I have been accused (often rightly so) of doing analytics that is too advanced, and no one understands what it means, no one understands how to use it. This is after I have done it, shown the results and put together a PowerPoint presentation explaining what it is and how it helps. It was typically the nature of my job to do a project and then, basically, go away. Theodore Levitt (who, it could be argued, basically invented marketing as a discipline with his 'Marketing myopia' article) said that people do not want a one-inch drill; they want to make a hole, one inch wide. I was often guilty of expounding on the coolness of the drill, the wonderful details and specifications of the drill, how the drill would help make a hole, why this drill is better than that drill, etc. I needed to focus on what was the need, not the tool. Therefore I'd suggest some of the following after analytics has been done.

Set up tactical use cases. Put together scenarios of before and after, with and without the analytics.

Train the staff, maybe even with real data. Design simulations or use past data and show how the analytics will be implemented. This may mean designing a tracking report and focusing on the new metrics. It ought to mean actually showing data, the score on the database and the strategic implications of the new insights. Take away the abstract black box: analytics is not voodoo.

Get stakeholders together and talk about their goals (especially those their bonuses are dependent on). Show how the new analytics directly impacts these metrics, and then decide upon stretch goals. I have typically found the bar is rather low. Most firms, even Fortune 100 firms, have little idea what's going on, have few insights and do not know their customers or competition. They typically market with a shotgun approach and throw money around hoping for the best. A few well-designed analytic projects can drastically make a difference. That's how you become a superstar.

You should set up check-ins at 30 days after, 90 days after, and 180 days after, etc, to get back together and see how it's going, what has been happening. You are a consultant and are there to help answer questions, ensure the modes are working and are being used correctly.

It's common to set up test vs control groups, so make sure you are part of this. Remember, everyone wants to test, but almost no one knows how to design a statistical test.

Find a way to make analytics central to as many divisions and senior people as possible. Get in front of as many decision makers as feasible. Never talk about the technical aspects of the analytics, always talk about the downstream resultant (typically financial) metrics. Instead of saying the t-ratio is significant and positive, tell them that net profit can increase by 2.5% next quarter. That will make them put their phones down and listen.

Take a class or read a book (or two) on abnormal psychology

Success in the corporate world depends more on your ability to work with people and get them to do what needs to be done than on your technical skills. This book has been about adding tools but really you need to understand people. Everyone is different, the same things do not work on all people, and people evolve and change over time.

All business emotions come from either fear or greed. Discover the primary motivator of the people above you and the people below you. Generally speaking, lower-level folks are tactic-oriented; they need a list of tasks to complete. As they rise in the corporate ranks they tend to become less tactical and more strategic. This means, generally, lower-level folks are motivated by fear (did they get the job done, was it done correctly, can they be blamed?) and higher-level people are motivated by greed (they run the organization and get a bonus, they get perks, newspaper clippings mention their name). As they reach a very high level they are motivated again by fear because they can be blamed for everything.

So you need to know people enough (especially those under you) so that you understand if they are going through a divorce, having trouble with their kids, drug problems, or just plain crazy. Some people would prefer recognition to a raise, a flexible schedule to an increase in title, one-on-one time with you instead of the forced frivolities of department off-sites. (BTW, not everyone loves bowling or paint ball!) So, invest and discover.

Consumer behaviour is predictable enough

What marketing science deals with is quantifying causality. That is, measuring how one variable impacts another variable. This means predicting consumer behaviour.

I like to point out that the weatherman, every day, predicts the weather. Every day it's wrong. (Maybe it's right enough, but you decide how often you have made fun of the bad predictions.) Meteorologists have decades of data and use mainframe computers to develop models. The data they deal with are dew points, temperature, wind, pressure, precipitation, etc. That is, they deal with inanimate objects. All of this, and they still can't get it right!

We marketing science folks typically have only a handful of years of data to work with. We do this on a PC or so, maybe a server. And we deal with irrational animate consumers. We have no chance to be 'right'.

But the techniques you've seen here help and they help to get it right often enough. It's often enough to move the needle on a corporation's financial performance. And by the way, how good does the model have to be? I've had a manager not use a model because it was not 100% accurate. (Yes, he was an idiot.)

I like to use the analogy of the evolution of the human eye. Millions of years ago our ancestors were blind and at high risk among predators. Eventually some mutations formed and we developed an 'eye bud' that allowed not perfect vision but could detect light from dark, could sense shadowy movements ahead, etc. I propose that while this eye bud was nowhere near perfect (not 100%) the insight (get it, sight?) was enough to allow them to make smarter decisions. Its visual acuity would grow and develop over time but at least it could now slightly 'see' large creatures coming toward it, it could tell day from night, maybe find food easier, etc. I propose this was enough to survive.

So, aim high. We came out of the mud.

The bar is low. We can only go up from here. Go get 'em!

GLOSSARY

Average: the most representative measure of central tendency, NOT necessarily the mean.

Censored observation: that observation wherein we do not know its status. Typically the event has not occurred yet or was lost in some way.

Collinearity: a measure of how variables are correlated with each other.

Correlation: a measure of both strength and direction, calculated as the covariance of X and Y divided by the standard deviation of X* the standard deviation of Y.

Covariance: the dispersion or spread of two variables.

Design of experiments: an inductive way of creating a statistical test using a stimulus taking into account variance, confidence, etc, by randomization and comparison to a control group.

Elastic demand: a place on the demand curve where a change in an input variable produces more than that change in an output variable.

Elasticity: a metric with no scale or dimension, calculated as the per cent change in an output variable given a per cent change in an input variable.

Inelastic demand: a place on the demand curve where a change in an input variable produces less than that change in an output variable.

Lift/gains chart: a visual device to aid in interpreting how a model performs. It compares by deciles the model's predictive power to random.

Maximum likelihood: an estimation technique (as opposed to ordinary least squares) that finds estimators that maximize the likelihood function observing the sample given.

Mean: a descriptive statistic, a measure of central tendency, the mean is a calculation summing up the value of all the observations and dividing by the number of observations.

Median: the middle observation in an odd number of observations, or the mean of the middle two observations.

Mode: the number that appears most often.

Ordinary regression: a statistical technique whereby a dependent variable depends on the movement of one or more independent variables (plus an error term).

Over sampling: a sampling technique forcing a particular metric to be over represented (larger) in the sample than in simple random sampling. This is done because a simple random sample would produce too few of that particular metric.

Range: a measure of dispersion or spread, calculated as the maximum value less the minimum value.

Reduced form equations: in econometrics, models solved in terms of endogenous variables.

Segmentation: a marketing strategy aimed at dividing the market into sub-markets, wherein each member in each segment is very similar by some measure to each other and very dissimilar to members in all other segments; in marketing strategy, a method of sub-dividing the population into similar sub-markets for better targeting, etc.

Simultaneous equations: a system of more than one dependent variable-type equation, often sharing several independent variables.

Standard deviation: the square root of variance.

Standard error: an estimate of standard deviation, calculated as the standard deviation divided by the square root of the number of observations.

Stratifying: a sampling technique choosing observations based on the distribution of another metric. This is done to ensure the sample contains adequate observations of that particular metric.

Variance: a measure of spread, calculated as the summed square of each observation less the mean, divided by the count of observations less one.

Z-score: a metric describing how many standard deviations an observation is from its mean.

BIBLIOGRAPHY AND FURTHER READING

Ariely, Dan (2008) *Predictably Irrational: The hidden forces that shape our decisions*, HarperCollins

Bagozzi, Richard P (ed) (1994) *Advanced Methods of Marketing Research*, Blackwell

Baier, Martin, Ruf, Kurtis and Chakraborty, Goutam (2002) *Contemporary Database Marketing: Concepts and applications*, Racom Communications

Becker, Gary (1962) Irrational behaviour and economic theory, *Journal of Political Economy*, **70** (1), pp 1–13

Belsley, David, Kuh, Edwin and Welsch, Roy (1980) *Regression Diagnostics: Identifying influential data and sources of collinearity*, John Wiley and Sons

Binger, Brian and Hoffman, Elizabeth (1998) *Microeconomics with Calculus*, Addison Wesley

Birn, Robin J (2009) *The Effective Use of Market Research: How to drive and focus better business decisions*, Kogan Page

Brown, William S (1991) *Introducing Econometrics*, West Publishing Company

Chiang, Alpha (1984) *Fundamental Methods of Mathematical Economics*, McGraw Hill

Cox, David (1972) Regression models and life tables, *Journal of the Royal Statistical Society*, **34** (2), pp 187–220

Deaton, Angus and Muellbauer, John (1980) *Economics and Consumer Behavior*, Cambridge University Press

Egan, Mary, Manfred, Kate, Bascle, Ivan, Huet, Emmanuel and Marcil, Sharon (2009) *The Consumer's Voice: Can your company hear it?* Boston Consulting Group, Center for Consumer Insights Benchmarking 2009 [online] available at: https://www.bcg.com/documents/file35167.pdf [accessed 30 October 2017]

Engel, James, Blackwell, Roger and Miniard, Paul (1995) *Consumer Behavior*, Dryden Press

Greene, William H (1993) *Econometric Analysis*, Prentice Hall

Grigsby, Mike (2002) Modeling elasticity, *Canadian Journal of Marketing Research*, **20** (2), p 72

Grigsby, Mike (2014) Rethinking RFM, *Marketing Insights*, March, p 22 onwards

Hair, Joseph, Anderson, Rolph, Tatham, Ronald and Black, William (1998) *Multivariate Data Analysis*, Prentice Hall

Hamburg, Morris (1987) *Statistical Analysis for Decision Making*, Harcourt Brace Jovanovich

Hazlitt, Henry (1979) *Economics in One Lesson: The shortest and surest way to understand basic economics*, Crown Publishers

Hughes, Arthur M (1996) *The Complete Database Marketer*, McGraw Hill

Information Week (2005) *SmartAdvice: The New Face of Project Management* [online] available at: https://www.informationweek.com/smartadvice-the-new-face-of-project-management/d/d-id/1035671 [accessed 30 October 2017]

Intriligator, Michael D, Bodkin, Ronald G and Hsiao, Cheng (1996) *Econometric Models, Techniques and Applications*, Prentice Hall

Jackson, Rob and Wang, Paul (1997) *Strategic Database Marketing*, NTC Business Books

Kachigan, Sam (1991) *Multivariate Statistical Analysis: A conceptual introduction*, Radius Press

Kennedy, Peter (1998) *A Guide to Econometrics*, MIT Press

Kmenta, Jan (1986) *Elements of Econometrics*, Macmillan

Kotler, Philip (1967) *Marketing Management: Analysis, planning and control*, Prentice Hall

Kotler, Philip (1989) From mass marketing to mass customization, *Planning Review*, **17** (5), pp 10–47

Lancaster, Kelvin (1971) *Consumer Demand*, Columbia University Press

Leeflang, Peter, SH, Wittink, Dick, Wedel, Michel and Naert, Philippe (2000) *Building Models for Marketing Decisions*, Kluwer Academic Publishers

Levitt, Theodore (1960) Marketing myopia, *Harvard Business Review*, **38**, pp 24–47

Lilien, Gary, Kotler, Philip and Moorthy, K Sridhar (2002) *Marketing Models*, Prentice-Hall International editions

Lindsay, Cotton Mather (1982) *Applied Price Theory*, Dryden Press

MacQueen, James B (1967) Some methods for classification and analysis of multivariate observations, in *Proceedings of 5th Berkeley Symposium on Mathematical Statistics and Probability*, University of California Press

Magidson, Jay and Vermunt, Jeroen (2002) A nontechnical introduction to latent class models, *Statistical Innovations*, white paper [online] http://statisticalinnovations.com/technicalsupport/lcmodels2.pdf

Magidson, Jay and Vermunt, Jeroen (2002) Latent class models for clustering: a comparison with K-means, *Canadian Journal of Marketing Research*, **20**, pp 37–44

Myers, James H (1996) *Segmentation and Positioning for Strategic Marketing Decisions*, American Marketing Association

Porter, Michael (1979) How competitive forces shape strategy, *Harvard Business Review*, March/April, pp 137–45

Porter, Michael (1980) *Competitive Strategy*, The Free Press

Rich, David, McCarthy, Brian and Harris, Jeanne (2009) *Getting Serious about Analytics: Better insights, better outcomes*, Accenture [online] available at: http://www.umsl.edu/~sauterv/DSS/Accenture_Getting_Serious_About_Analytics.pdf [accessed 30 October 2017]

Samuelson, Paul (1947) *Foundations of Economic Analysis*, Harvard University Press

Schnaars, Steven P (1997) *Marketing Strategy: Customers & competition*, The Free Press

Silberberg, Eugene (1990) *The Structure of Economics: A mathematical analysis*, McGraw Hill

Sorger, Stephan (2013) *Marketing Analytics*, Admiral Press

Stone, Merlin, Bond, Alison and Foss, Bryan (2004) *Consumer Insight: How to use data and market research to get closer to your customer*, Kogan Page

Sudman, Seymour and Blair, Edward (1998) *Marketing Research: A problem solving approach*, McGraw Hill

Takayama, Akira (1993) *Analytical Methods in Economics*, University of Michigan Press

Treacy, Michael and Wiersema, Fred (1997) *The Discipline of Market Leaders: Choose your customers, narrow your focus, dominate your market*, Addison Wesley

Urban, Glen L and Star, Steven H (1991) *Advanced Marketing Strategy: Phenomena, analysis and decisions*, Prentice Hall

Varian, Hal (1992) *Microeconomic Analysis*, W.W. Norton & Company

Wedel, Michel and Kamakura, Wagner A (1998) *Market Segmentation: Conceptual and methodological foundations*, Kluwer Academic Publishers

Weinstein, Art (1994) *Market Segmentation: Using demographics, psychographics and other niche marketing techniques to predict and model customer behavior*, Irwin Professional Publishing

INDEX